DIARY OF MY SONGS
[JOURNAL DE MES MÉLODIES]

Poulenc and Bernac

FRANCIS POULENC

DIARY OF MY SONGS

[JOURNAL DE MES MÉLODIES]

With a translation by

WINIFRED RADFORD

Foreword by Graham Johnson

KAHN & AVERILL

This edition first published in 2006 by
Kahn & Averill
9 Harrington Road, London SW17 3ES.

Originally published in French, in a limited edition,
by Éditions Bernard Grasset, Paris, 1964.

This bilingual edition first published in Great Britain
in 1985 by Victor Gollancz Ltd,

Journal de mes mélodies © 1964 by Éditions Bernard Grasset
English translation © Winifred Radford 1985
Foreword © Graham Johnson 1985
Notes © Winifred Radford & Patrick Saul 1985
Bibliography and Discographical Appendix © Patrick Saul 1985

Pubication of the 1985 edition was made possible by a
grant from Les Amis de Francis Poulenc, Paris,
who also provided the photographs, some of which are
reproduced by courtesy of Mme Rose Dercourt-Plaut.

British Library Cataloguing in Publication Data
A catalogue record for this book is available from the British Library

ISBN 1-871082-86-2

Printed in Great Britain by
Halstan & Co Ltd, Amersham, Bucks.

NOTE ON THE TRANSLATOR

Winifred Radford, daughter of the celebrated English bass, Robert Radford, made her initial appearance in opera at the first Glyndebourne Festival in 1934. She also toured with *Intimate* Opera and gave song recitals and frequent broadcasts, specialising in French song. In 1945 she gave the first performance in England of Poulenc's song cycle *Fiançailles pour rire,* coached by Francis Poulenc and Pierre Bernac. Subsequently she studied intensively with Bernac, with whom she was associated in the production of two books, *The Interpretation of French Song and Francis Poulenc, the Man and his Songs.* From 1955-71 she taught singing at the Guildhall School of Music and Drama where she established a class for the Interpretation of French Song. After retiring she concentrated on private teaching. Winifred Radford died in 1993.

Winifred Radford and Pierre Bernac at Fontainebleau in 1947.

CONTENTS

NOTE

An asterisk in the English text refers to an
entry in the Discographical Appendix.

Capitalization in the French text follows the
style of the original edition; capitalization
elsewhere follows modern practice.

LIST OF ILLUSTRATIONS

FOREWORD

to the English Edition

by

GRAHAM JOHNSON

THE REAPPEARANCE OF this little book will be welcomed by seasoned French song *aficionados* who will note the addition of a helpful parallel translation and rare photographs. But up to now, younger music lovers have not had the opportunity to own a copy of Poulenc's song diary. Since the limited edition, privately printed by Les Amis de Francis Poulenc, appeared in 1964, a new generation has fallen in love with his music. Among Poulenc's fans are English-speaking singers who are too young to have heard Pierre Bernac in recital, and accompanists (myself among their number) who missed hearing the composer play his own songs. This book fills in some of the gaps across that national and time divide, which even gramophone records can only partially bridge.

Posthumous judgement has firmly decided that Poulenc is more than a *petit maître*; the size of his heart and the sincerity of his song have earned him a place beside the other immortals of the *mélodie*. For it is Poulenc's vocal music in particular which is increasingly regarded as his very best work. I confess that my love for it has something to do with the fact that it captures the atmosphere of an epoch that I am furious to have missed. Poulenc has caught the essential flavour of those times — thirty, forty, fifty years ago. Listen to (one could almost say taste) certain Poulenc songs and Paris returns in a flash, not Proust's *Belle Époque* Paris but a generation later, the stamping-ground of Cocteau and Picasso, the site of Max Jacob's slum and Marie-Blanche de Polignac's salon.

Poulenc's songs documented the twenties and thirties from within. For those of us born in the fifties, he has even given the

13

late forties an aura of glamour. It is all to be found in this book — indeed Poulenc's prose style bears a great resemblance to his music. Flashes of acerbic wit and world-weary cynicism are balanced by lyrical passages which come straight from the heart but which never descend to sentimentality. In the writing of words as in the writing of music, economy and effusion, precision and mysterious fantasy go together in a combination unique to this composer. In his frivolity there is that trace of inconsolable melancholy that is a perpetual part of his work. When we read the writings of Schumann and Debussy we can also hear the spirit of their music somehow translated into prose. Poulenc belonged to that small group of composers who were able to leave important clues to their musical style by non-musical means.

Poulenc was proud of his *mélodies*, just as he was proud of his knowledge of twentieth-century French literature, his exceptional feeling for prosody and his friendship with a number of his poets. The pleasure he took in this branch of his output, however, was by no means a sign of self-satisfaction. Indeed, he was hard on himself to the point of suffering bouts of depression over his music — the same music which is nevertheless often performed and much loved throughout the world. This charming, gregarious and yet infinitely complex man (both "ragamuffin" and "monk" as Claude Rostand described his two-sided musical personality) was often un-happy with himself. He was only too aware, for example, that he was lazy: he did not relish submitting himself to the systematic discipline necessary to compose. Those who knew him say it was a miracle that he wrote as much as he did. (There is surely a lesson here: the man fighting against his tendency to do little, in the end probably achieves more than the industrious drone, proud of his industry.) Two slim volumes of prose show that our "idle" composer could also put pen to paper (ordinary paper not music manuscript), when affection moved him to do so. The book on Chabrier, Poulenc's "Grand-papa" — more evocation than biography — was his love-offering to the past; the *Journal de mes mélodies* a

bequest to the future. I believe he wrote it because he feared that the passing of time would render his cherished songs less accessible to later generations who could not be expected to understand the allusions and atmosphere that he and his contemporaries took for granted. The notes to this edition and the splendidly informative discography bring these allusions into even sharper focus.

In 1985 we find ourselves increasingly distanced from the world Poulenc inhabited. We mourn the composition of *mélodies* as a lost art. We are fortunate that the writings and teaching of Pierre Bernac have provided a firm basis for a continuing understanding of Poulenc's style. There is also a marvellous legacy of Bernac–Poulenc performances on gramophone records which have never been bettered. But this *Journal* is perhaps the most unusual part of the Poulenc legacy, for in words rather than music it suggests the poetic, idiosyncratic, unpredictable workings of a great composer's mind and heart. No other creator of songs has left us such a book — it is an indispensable document.

On behalf of my generation of British musicians, I salute the indefatigable Winifred Radford who has brought *Journal de mes mélodies* once more before the public. Pierre Bernac served his chosen composer with hard work and devotion for over 25 years. He is the behind-the-scenes hero of this journal; in Winifred he found as devoted a disciple and friend for his work as he had been for Poulenc's. The considerable influence on English and American recital programmes, singing and music-making which Poulenc's work now enjoys is due in no small measure to Bernac and Radford. It is an utterly fitting arrangement that the Friends of Poulenc in France and the Friends of Bernac in England should have joined forces to produce this bi-lingual edition.

LONDON 1985   G. J.

AVANT-PROPOS

[PREFACE TO THE ORIGINAL EDITION]

par

HENRI SAUGUET

CES LIGNES QUE vous allez lire, il n'a tenu qu'au destin de Francis Poulenc qu'elles deviennent posthumes: tout, dans cet écrit, témoigne de la vie même de celui qui le traça pour non point tant qu'on le lise mais plus encore qu'on le consulte. Ces pages sont intimément liées à ses œuvres vocales dont on sait l'importance dans son œuvre et par la place qu'elles occupent dans la musique vocale de notre temps.

Francis Poulenc était extrêmement vigilant des interprétations de sa musique; on verra ici ce que celle-ci lui a coûté de soins et donné de soucis dans son apparente simplicité. Le musicien appartenait à cette race d'êtres qui entendent ne pas cacher leur pensée sous les richesses superflues et les signes extérieurs des complications d'écriture. La simplification des signes, chez lui, est bien davantage volonté de rigueur qu'abandon. Et c'est bien ce qui fait le prix de ces pages révélatrices, indicatrices et leur donne un ton, un intérêt, un poids qui les rendent voisines des journaux d'écrivain qui sont aujourd'hui si fréquentés pour tant de raisons.

L'Association des Amis de Francis Poulenc a voulu qu'une de ses premières manifestations soit liée à cette indispensable publication que les Éditions Bernard Grasset ont reçue dans leur illustre maison avec une grâce, une élégance, une générosité auxquelles nous voulons rendre un hommage reconnaissant. Par elles, le *Journal de mes mélodies* de Francis Poulenc, pourra atteindre tous ceux qui sont intéressés autant par la vie de l'artiste que par son art même.

MAI 1964   H. S.

THE DIARY

Horrible journée!!!

Une dame vient de miauler, un quart d'heure durant, à la radio des mélodies qui pourraient bien être de moi! Ah! les chanteuses qui n'écoutent que leur instinct. Je devrais dire leurs instincts car je suppose, celle-ci, douée pour tout autre chose que la musique. On massacre souvent mes pièces de piano mais jamais tant que mes mélodies et, Dieu sait, que je tiens plus à celles-ci qu'à celles-là.

J'entreprends ce Journal dans l'espoir de servir de guide aux interprètes qui auraient quelque souci de ma pauvre musique. Je devrais écrire misérable car, telle elle m'est apparue, chantée ainsi.

Si j'étais professeur de chant j'obligerais mes élèves à *lire attentivement les poèmes* avant de travailler une mélodie.

La plupart du temps ces dames et ces messieurs ne comprennent pas un mot de ce qu'ils chantent.

Je me souviens d'une chanteuse qui offrait, comme sur le carreau des halles, les fruits et les fleurs de « Green » de Debussy. Dans les vingt dernières mesures, la susdite dame quittait les « primeurs » pour le « rayon parfums ».

« L'accompagnement » d'un lied est aussi important que la partie de piano d'une sonate. Qui songerait à escamoter les traits du scherzo de la première sonate de Fauré.

November 3rd, 1939

What a horrible day!!!

On the radio a lady has just been caterwauling for a quarter of an hour some songs which may very well have been mine! Ah! singers who follow only their own instinct. I ought to say instincts, since I presume this lady to be gifted in quite other directions than music. My piano pieces are often massacred, but never to such an extent as my songs and, heaven knows, I place a higher value on the songs.

I am undertaking this diary in the hope that it will serve as a guide to those interpreters who feel some interest in my poor music. I ought to call it miserable music, for that is how it appeared to me, sung in this way.

November 7th, 1939

If I were a singing teacher I would insist on my pupils *reading the poems attentively* before working at a song.

Most of the time these ladies and gentlemen do not understand a word of what they are singing.

I remember a singer who offered the fruit and flowers of 'Green'[1] by Debussy as though from a stall in the market. In the last twenty bars, the aforesaid lady left the "fresh produce" for the "perfumery counter".

November 9th, 1939

"The accompaniment" of a song is as important as the piano part of a sonata. Who would dream of fudging the brilliant passages in the scherzo of the first sonata of Fauré?[2]

11 novembre 1939

LE BESTIAIRE

Mes premières mélodies composées en 1918, à Pont-sur-Seine. Je venais de connaître Apollinaire chez Valentine Hugo. Le cycle comprenait originairement douze mélodies. Je n'en ai gardé que six sur le conseil d'Auric. A Pont-sur-Seine j'étais soldat. En arrivant en permission à Paris: stupeur de constater que Louis Durey avait eu la même idée que moi et avait mis en musique *tout Le Bestiaire.* Du coup je lui ai dédié le mien.

Ces courtes mélodies sont originalement composées pour voix et orchestre de chambre.

On les a tant entendues au piano qu'on l'oublie. C'est dommage. Chanter LE BESTIAIRE avec ironie et surtout des *intentions* est un contresens complet. C'est ne rien comprendre à la poésie d'Apollinaire et à ma musique. Je garde précieusement une lettre de Marie Laurencin qui trouve que mes mélodies ont le « son de voix de Guillaume »; pas de plus beau compliment. Il a fallu que Marya Freund chante LE BESTIAIRE aussi gravement que du Schubert pour qu'on comprenne que c'était mieux qu'une blague. Je m'étonne parfois que ces premières mélodies soient déjà « très Poulenc ». Je n'en dirai pas autant des POÈMES DE RONSARD écrits six ans plus tard. C'est d'ailleurs un cas assez fréquent de voir une personnalité qui s'affirme à ses débuts, puis s'égare. Qui peut admettre sans surprise que les *Ariettes oubliées* de Debussy sont antérieures aux *Poèmes de Baudelaire.*

Dès LE BESTIAIRE j'ai senti un lien, un lien, sûr et mystérieux, avec la poésie d'Apollinaire.

LA CARPE n'a rien à voir avec Fontainebleau. Je l'ai esquissée dans un wagon-restaurant, entre Longueville et Paris.

Les COCARDES datent de la même époque. Elles sont écrites sous l'influence orchestrale de Stravinsky, bien que cela soit moins

November 11th, 1939

LE BESTIAIRE
[THE BOOK OF BEASTS]

My first songs composed in 1918, at Pont-sur-Seine. I had recently met Apollinaire★ at Valentine Hugo's.[3] The cycle originally consisted of twelve songs. On the advice of Auric★ I kept only six. At Pont-sur-Seine I was in the army. Arriving in Paris on leave I learned to my amazement that Louis Durey★ had had the same idea as I had and had set *all Le Bestiaire*. At once I dedicated mine to him.

These short songs were originally composed for voice and chamber orchestra.

They are so often heard with piano that the original has been forgotten. That's a pity. To sing *Le Bestiaire* with irony and above all *knowingly* is a complete misconception, showing no understanding whatsoever of Apollinaire's poetry or my music. I treasure a letter from Marie Laurencin[4] saying that my songs had the "sound of Guillaume's voice"; there could be no finer compliment. It needed Marya Freund★ to sing *Le Bestiaire* as gravely as a song by Schubert[5] to prove that it is something better than a piece of nonsense. At times I am astonished that these first songs are already "typical Poulenc". I will not say as much for the *Poèmes de Ronsard* written six years later. It is not unusual, however, to see a personality asserting itself at the beginning and then going astray. Who can accept without surprise that the *Ariettes oubliées* of Debussy are earlier than the *Poèmes de Baudelaire*?[6]

Ever since *Le Bestiaire* I have felt a definite and mysterious affinity with the poetry of Apollinaire.

'La Carpe' has no connection with Fontainebleau.[7] I sketched it out in a restaurant-car between Longueville and Paris.

The *Cocardes* date from the same period. They were written under the orchestral influence of Stravinsky,★ though that is

visible ici qu'ailleurs et sous l'influence esthétique, tricolore, de Roger de la Fresnaye.

On doit également chanter ce cycle sans ironie. L'essentiel, c'est de croire aux mots qui s'envolent comme un oiseau, d'une branche à une autre.

Médrano de 1920, Paris d'avant 1914 (la bande à Bonnot, quoi!), Marseille de 1918 sont évoqués ici. Il s'agit de les deviner, comme ces vues qu'on regarde dans un porte-plume.

Je range COCARDES dans mes « œuvres Nogent » avec une odeur de frites, d'accordéon, de parfum Piver. En un mot tout ce que j'ai aimé à cet âge et que j'aime encore. Pourquoi pas?

CINQ POÈMES DE RONSARD écrits après *Les Biches* avec toutes les négligences possibles sauf, Dieu merci, de prosodie. Le premier poème est assez réussi avec une grande influence de *Mavra*. Certains de mes confrères ont chanté les louanges de ce recueil, à sa parution. Sans doute parce qu'aimant peu ma musique, ils étaient heureux de me retrouver ici, moins exactement moi-même. Auric, lui, ne s'y est pas trompé. J'ai souvenir d'une nuit de mars, dans la gare de Meudon. Nous revenions de chez un ami. En attendant le train il me démontra en deux secondes que ce n'était pas là ma vraie nature, en dépit des dernières pages d'A SON PAGE et de certains coins de BALLET (je le cite).

On doit chanter ATTRIBUTS imperturbablement, sans aucun *rubato*. L'interprétation des autres mélodies est sans surprise . . . comme la musique.

CHANSONS GAILLARDES

Je tiens à ce recueil où j'ai tâché de démontrer, que l'obscénité peut s'accommoder de la musique. Je déteste la grivoiserie. Les

less obvious here than elsewhere, and under the aesthetic influence, very French, of Roger de la Fresnaye.[8]

This cycle, too, must be sung without irony. The essential point is to believe in the words which fly like a bird from one branch to another.

Médrano[9] in 1920, Paris before 1914 (Bonnot's gang!),[10] Marseilles in 1918 are evoked here. It is a matter of trying to discern them, like views you look at in a pen-holder. I class *Cocardes* among my "Nogent[11] works" with the smell of chips, the accordion, Piver perfume. In a word, all that I loved at that age and that I still love. Why not?

Cinq Poèmes de Ronsard written after *Les Biches*[12] with all possible carelessness, except, thank goodness, over the prosody. The first poem is successful enough, greatly influenced by *Mavra*.[13] Certain of my colleagues sang the praises of this collection when it appeared, doubtless because, not liking my music much, they were happy to find me here less entirely myself. But Auric made no mistake about it. I remember a night in March, in the station at Meudon. We were returning from a visit to a friend. Waiting for the train, he proved to me in two seconds that my true nature was not in these songs, despite the last pages of 'A son page' and certain places in 'Ballet' (I am quoting him).

'Attributs' should be sung imperturbably, without any *rubato*. The interpretation of the other songs is nothing unusual . . . like the music.

CHANSONS GAILLARDES
[RIBALD SONGS]

I am fond of this collection where I tried to show that outright obscenity can adapt itself to music. I detest smutty suggestive-

accompagnements sont très difficiles mais bien écrits, je crois. Trouvé les textes dans une Anthologie de chanson du xviiᵉ siècle (édition ancienne).

L'Invocation aux parques serait de . . . Racine.

Les Couplets bachiques et La belle jeunesse doivent se jouer *très vite*. L'accompagnement avec la précision d'une étude pour piano.

AIRS CHANTÉS

Moi qui suis si peu fait pour le paradoxe, il faut pour cela la maîtrise de Ravel, je m'étonne toujours d'avoir pu écrire ces quatre mélodies. Je déteste Moréas et j'ai choisi justement ses poèmes parce que je les trouvais propices à la mutilation. Dans L'Air champêtre j'ai pu faire admettre « sous la mou, sous la mousse à moitié ». Ai-je été puni de mon vandalisme? Je le crains car cette mélodie qui m'irrite est dite « à succès ».

La première mélodie Air romantique doit se chanter très vite, le vent dans la figure. Le *tempo* doit être implacable.

L'Air grave est d'un poncif indéfendable.

L'Air vif à chanter très vite également, dans une explosion de joie, est le type de la fausse réussite.

ÉPITAPHE

Croquis sur un beau poème de Malherbe. J'ai pensé en l'écrivant à une architecture Louis XIII. A chanter *sans emphase*.

ness. The accompaniments are very difficult but well written, I think. The texts were found in an anthology of songs of the 17th century (an old edition).

'Invocation aux Parques' might be by . . . Racine.[14]

'Couplets bachiques' and 'La belle jeunesse' must be performed *very fast*. The accompaniment should have the precision of an *étude* for piano.

AIRS CHANTÉS

I, who am so little gifted for paradox — for that the mastery of Ravel[15] is needed — I am always astonished at myself for having been able to write these four songs. I detest Moréas[16] and I chose these poems precisely because I found them suitable for mutilation. In 'Air champêtre' I have actually permitted "sous la mou, sous la mousse à moitié". Have I been punished for my vandalism? I fear so, because this song that irritates me is said to be "a hit".

The first song, 'Air romantique', must be sung very fast, with the wind in one's face. The *tempo* must be implacable.

'Air grave' is indefensibly conventional.

'Air vif', which should also be sung very fast, in an explosion of joy, is typical of a spurious success.

ÉPITAPHE

Sketched to a beautiful poem by Malherbe.[17] While writing it my thoughts were of Louis XIII architecture. To be sung *without bombast*.

TROIS POÈMES DE LOUISE LALANNE
(Apollinaire)

C'est avec Apollinaire que je pense avoir trouvé mon véritable style mélodique. Ces mélodies sont difficiles, même la dernière. On commet généralement une faute rythmique en n'admettant pas, dans LE PRÉSENT, la stricte égalité des doubles croches du début. J'aurais pu écrire le tout à 2/4 en mesurant de ce fait les blancs des premières mesures. Il m'a semblé pourtant plus sensible d'écrire un 3/8 suivi d'une respiration. C'est à la chanteuse de donner l'impression d'intensité d'un souffle court. La mélodie doit couler sans l'ombre d'un *rubato*. Influencé par l'écriture à l'unisson du final de la Sonate de Chopin.

Le rythme de la seconde doit être imperturbable. J'entends cela comme la chanson à compter: « Am — stram — gram — pic et pic et colégram. »

HIER. J'ai songé en l'écrivant à un intérieur peint par Vuillard. Si l'on pense bien aux mots que l'on dit, la couleur viendra d'elle-même.

Louise Lalanne n'a jamais existé, c'est le fruit d'une mystification d'Apollinaire. HIER est d'ailleurs de Marie Laurencin.

Composé en même temps les QUATRE POÈMES D'APOLLINAIRE.

Prédilection pour L'ANGUILLE qui sent l'hôtel borgne, est rythmé à petits pas de chaussons de feutre et devrait *émouvoir*. Chanter cette mélodie sans ironie, en y croyant. Le mot « *dimanche* » vient si bien dans le poème!

CARTE POSTALE — rythme imperturbable: pensé à Misia Sert au piano, peinte par Bonnard. Souligner l'intimité de cette mélodie.

AVANT LE CINÉMA à chanter également tout droit.

TROIS POÈMES DE LOUISE LALANNE
[THREE POEMS BY LOUISE LALANNE]
(Apollinaire)

It is with Apollinaire that I think I have found my true melodic style. These songs are difficult, even the last one. People generally make a rhythmic mistake in 'Le Présent'[18] by not allowing the semiquavers at the beginning to be strictly equal. I could have written the whole song in 2/4, adjusting the rests in the first bars. However, it seemed to me more acute to write in 3/8 followed by a catch of the breath. It is for the singer to give an impression of intensity by slight breathlessness. The song must flow without the shadow of a *rubato*. It is influenced by the writing in unison at the end of the Chopin Sonata.

The rhythm of the second must be imperturbable. I think of it as a counting song: "Am — stram — gram — pic et pic et colégram".

'Hier'. While writing it I imagined an interior painted by Vuillard.[19] If you think carefully of the words you are saying, the colour will come of itself.

Louise Lalanne never existed — she is the result of a hoax by Apollinaire. Moreover 'Hier' is by Marie Laurencin.

The *Quatre Poèmes d'Apollinaire* were composed at the same time. I have a predilection for 'L'Anguille' which evokes the atmosphere of a shady hotel, with a rhythm inspired by little steps in felt shoes, and should be *touching*. Sing this song without irony, believing in it. The word "dimanche" comes so effectively in the poem!

'Carte postale' — imperturbable rhythm: think of Misia Sert at the piano, painted by Bonnard.[20] Emphasize the intimacy of this song.

1904. Combien j'aime ce kaléidoscope de mots. Colette m'a fait remarquer, dans la première édition, une coquille, commune au volume *Il y a* d'où ce poème est tiré. Lire « Hébé *qui* les dieux servait » et non *que* les dieux servaient.

Ne pas souligner exagérément le côté repu et érotique de la chute finale. Ce qui est noté musicalement suffit déjà.

Roger Bourdin qui a créé ce recueil, y était excellent.

CINQ POÈMES DE MAX JACOB

Sortes de tableaux bretons. Mélodies avant tout descriptives.

La première CHANSON est très difficile à interpréter. C'est la place de Guidel en Bretagne, un matin d'été. Une paysanne conte, très simplement, ses infortunes.

La dernière page brusquement devient poétique et irréelle. Des oiseaux chantent sur le bord d'un chemin.

CIMETIÈRE sent la couronne de perles qu'on achète chez l'épicier. L'ensemble est un peu chromo. Chanter cela tout droit.

LA PETITE SERVANTE. Très directement inspiré de Moussorgsky. La description des maux redoutés doit être débitée strictement et nerveusement. La fin, l'archet à la corde.

BERCEUSE. Tout étant à rebours dans le poème: le père à la messe, la mère au cabaret, un rythme de valse tient lieu de berceuse. Cela sent le cidre et l'odeur âcre des chaumières.

SOURIC ET MOURIC. Le début d'un débit très rapide, toujours dans le style d'une chanson à compter (Am stram gram). Si l'on ne presse pas, avec souplesse, sur les mots: « *des pommiers pour la saison* » l'enchaînement de la conclusion ne peut pas se produire sans heurts et *il ne doit pas y avoir* de heurts.

J'avoue ma prédilection pour les deux dernières pages qui donnent je crois une véritable impression de nuit.

'Avant le cinéma' — again to be sung quite straight-forwardly.

'1904'. How much I like this kaleidoscope of words! Colette[21] pointed out to me a misprint in the first edition of the volume *Il y a* from which this poem is taken. Read "Hébé *qui* les dieux servait" and not "Hébé *que* les dieux servaient".

Do not over-emphasize the sated, erotic aspect of the final cadence. It is sufficiently expressed in the music.

Roger Bourdin,★ who created this cycle, was excellent in it.

❧❧

CINQ POÈMES DE MAX JACOB
[FIVE POEMS BY MAX JACOB][22]

These are in the character of Breton scenes. The songs are first and foremost descriptive.

The first, 'Chanson', is very difficult to interpret. The scene is the market place of Guidel in Brittany one summer morning. A peasant girl recounts, very simply, her misfortunes.

The last page suddenly becomes poetic and unreal. Birds sing by the wayside.

'Cimetière' has the atmosphere of the artificial wreaths of pearls which can be bought at the grocer's. It's all a little like a garish colour print. Sing it quite straightforwardly.

'La Petite servante'. Directly inspired by Mussorgsky.[23] The description of the dreaded maladies must be pronounced precisely and vigorously. The end should be well "bowed".[24]

'Berceuse'. Everything is topsy-turvy in the poem: the father is at mass, the mother in a tavern, a waltz rhythm takes the place of a cradle song. It is redolent of cider and the acrid smell of the thatched cottages.

'Souric et Mouric'. The opening with very rapid delivery, throughout in the style of a counting song (Am stram gram). If there is not a feeling of urgency, combined with flexibility, at the words "*des pommiers pour la saison*" the chord progression at the conclusion will not come without a shock and *there must*

Composé ceci à Nogent où j'étais venu passer deux mois en 1931 dans ma maison d'enfance, toute vide mais pleine de souvenirs.

Je ne peux jouer cette mélodie sans penser à mon chien Mickey, couché sous le piano.

※

HUIT CHANSONS POLONAISES

Harmonisées à la demande de Modrakowska pour une tournée au Maroc. La dernière, LE LAC, est la plus réussie, la plus personnelle. Les autres sont un peu conventionnelles mais assez jolies comme piano. Après tout y avait-il autre chose à faire qu'à « improviser » un accompagnement? Evidemment les « Grecques » de Ravel sont du « Ravel malgré tout » mais outre que je ne suis pas Ravel (hélas!) celui-ci n'avait pas à redouter l'ombre d'un Chopin athénien.

Modrakowska chantait divinement tout ceci.

※

CINQ POÈMES D'ÉLUARD

Œuvre de tâtonnement. Clef tournée dans une serrure. Tentative pour faire rendre au piano le *maximum* avec le *minimum* de moyens. Beaucoup pensé en composant ces mélodies à une exposition de dessins de Matisse pour un livre de Mallarmé, où l'on voyait le même dessin, au crayon, plein de hachures, de redites et l'épreuve finale n'ayant retenu que l'essentiel, dans un seul jet de plume. Je regrette d'avoir brûlé le brouillon de PEUT-IL SE REPOSER. Un critique suisse qui ne me rate jamais pourrait voir d'où vient « mon écriture

be no shock here.

I confess my predilection for the last two pages which give, I believe, a true impression of night.

This was composed at Nogent where I was spending two months in 1931 in the house of my childhood, quite empty but full of memories. I cannot play this song without thinking of my dog Mickey, lying under the piano.

❧❧

HUIT CHANSONS POLONAISES
[EIGHT POLISH SONGS]

Harmonized at the request of Modrakowska★ for a tour in Morocco. The last one, 'Le Lac', is the most successful, the most personal. The others are a little conventional but nice enough for the piano. After all, was there anything to do other than to "improvise" an accompaniment? Obviously the *Greek Songs* of Ravel[15] are by "Ravel in spite of all" but apart from the fact that I am not Ravel (alas!) he did not have to fear the ghost of an Athenian Chopin.

Modrakowska sang all these divinely.

❧❧

CINQ POÈMES D'ÉLUARD
[FIVE POEMS BY ÉLUARD][25]

Feeling my way in this work. Key turned in the lock. Trying to give the piano the *maximum* with the *minimum* of means. While composing these songs I often thought of an exhibition of drawings by Matisse[26] for a book by Mallarmé,[27] where the same pencil drawing could be seen, full of hatching, of repetitions, finally retaining nothing but the essential, in a single stroke of a pen. I regret having burned the draft of 'Peut-il se reposer'. A Swiss critic[28] who never lets me get away with anything could see where my "simplistic writing"

simpliste ». C'est du piano décanté, voilà tout.

La seconde mélodie est horriblement difficile. Il faut bien connaître Éluard, car on doit *deviner* le tempo qu'aucun métronome ne peut préciser.

PLUME D'EAU CLAIRE et RÔDEUSE sont, je crois, les meilleures mélodies du recueil. J'avais cherché des années la clef musicale de la poésie d'Éluard. Ici elle grince, pour la première fois, dans la serrure. Je me souviens de ma joie lorsque j'ai trouvé la prosodie de « Ses yeux s'ajourent, rient très fort ». Phonétiquement « s'ajourent » pouvait prendre figure d'adjectif. Je crois avoir évité cet écueil.

Première audition à notre premier récital, avec Bernac salle de l'École Normale — le 3 avril 1935.

A SA GUITARE. Quelques vers de Ronsard pris dans un long poème à l'occasion d'une chanson composée pour Yvonne Printemps (dernier tableau de *Margot* d'Édouard Bourdet).

J'ai essayé ici d'éviter « *la couleur du temps* ». Pensé cependant à Plessis-les-Tours.

Yvonne Printemps a enregistré A SA GUITARE dans une version rehaussée de quelques touches instrumentales. J'ai perdu malheureusement le matériel. Je le regrette car c'était assez joli.

TEL JOUR TELLE NUIT

On ne saura jamais assez tout ce que je dois à Éluard, tout ce que je dois à Bernac. C'est grâce à eux que le lyrisme a pénétré

came from. It's the piano reduced to its essence, that's all.

The second song is terribly difficult. One needs to be familiar with Éluard's work, because the tempo, which no metronome can indicate exactly, must be felt instinctively.

◎◎

'Plume d'eau claire' and 'Rôdeuse' are, I think, the best songs of the collection. For years I had sought the musical key to the poetry of Éluard. Here, for the first time, it grates in the lock. I recall my joy when I found the prosody of "ses yeux s'ajourent, rient très fort". Phonetically "s'ajourent" could have represented an adjective. I think I have avoided this danger.

The first performance was at my first recital with Bernac★ in the hall of the École Normale — April 3rd, 1935.

◎◎

'A sa guitare'. Some lines taken from a long poem for a song composed for Yvonne Printemps★ (the last scene of *Margot* by Édouard Bourdet).[29] I have tried here to avoid a contrived period flavour, but thought nevertheless of Plessis-les-Tours.[30]

Yvonne Printemps has recorded 'A sa guitare' in a version enhanced by some instrumental additions. Unfortunately I have lost the score — a pity, because it was rather pleasing.

◎◎

TEL JOUR TELLE NUIT
[SUCH A DAY SUCH A NIGHT]

People will never know how much I owe to Éluard, how much I owe to Bernac. It is due to them that lyricism has

dans mon œuvre vocale.

Lorsque je reste des semaines à travailler loin de Paris c'est vraiment avec un cœur d'amoureux que je retrouve « ma ville ». Un dimanche de novembre 36, je me sentais parfaitement heureux flânant du côté de la Bastille. Je commençai à réciter le poème extrait des *Yeux fertiles: Bonne journée*. Le soir la musique venait toute seule.

J'estime qu'une mélodie de cycle doit avoir une couleur et une architecture spéciales.

Un numéro de mélodies variées de Fauré (même de la même époque) n'aura jamais l'unité de *La Bonne chanson*, par exemple.

C'est pourquoi j'ai ouvert et fermé TEL JOUR TELLE NUIT par deux mélodies de tons et de *tempi* semblables.

Il faut chanter BONNE JOURNÉE avec une joie *bien calme*.

UNE RUINE doit se chanter immuablement irréel. JE NOMMERAI TON FRONT,† UNE ROULOTTE et A TOUTES BRIDES sont strictement des mélodies de cycle qu'il me semble impossible de chanter séparément. Je crois bien avoir rencontré quelque part l'enfant de la roulotte, une fin d'après-midi de novembre à Ménilmontant.

A TOUTES BRIDES n'a d'autre prétention que de faire valoir UNE HERBE PAUVRE. Ce poème d'Éluard a pour moi un goût divin. Retrouvé en lui cette amertume vivifiante d'une fleur jadis cueillie et mâchée aux environs de la Grande Chartreuse.

JE N'AI ENVIE QUE DE T'AIMER. A chanter dans une seule courbe, un seul élan.

FIGURE DE FORCE est également une mélodie pour faire *entendre* l'espèce de silence qu'est le début de NOUS AVONS FAIT LA NUIT.

J'ai écrit cette mélodie dans l'émotion la plus sincère. J'espère que cela se perçoit. La *coda* pianistique est essentielle. La jouer dans un mouvement strict, sans se hâter (pour faire applaudir le chanteur).

Les dernières mesures tendent la main à BONNE JOURNÉE.

---

† NOTE DE L'ÉDITEUR: Il semble y avoir une erreur ici. Poulenc a voulu dire «Le Front comme un drapeau perdu». «Je nommerai ton front» a été publié plus tard.

entered my vocal works.

When I remain for weeks working far away from Paris it is indeed with a heart full of love that I return to "my town". One Sunday in November 1936, I was feeling perfectly happy strolling towards the Bastille.[31] I began to repeat the poem from *Les Yeux fertiles: Bonne journée*. In the evening the music came of itself.

In my estimation a song in a cycle must have a special colour and architecture.

A number of various songs by Fauré (even of the same period) will never have the unity of *La Bonne chanson*, for example.

This is why I have opened and closed *Tel jour telle nuit* with two songs in similar keys and *tempi*.

'Bonne journée' should be sung with *very peaceful* joy.

'Une ruine' must be sung with a sense of complete unreality. 'Je nommerai ton front'[41], 'Une Roulotte' and 'A toutes brides' are strictly songs from a cycle and, it seems to me, could not possibly be sung separately. I believe I saw the child of the gypsy wagon somewhere late one afternoon in November at Ménilmontant.[31]

'A toutes brides' has no other pretension than to heighten the effect of 'Une Herbe pauvre'. This poem of Éluard has for me a divine savour. It recalls for me that invigorating bitterness of a flower I once plucked and munched in the surroundings of the Grande Chartreuse.[32]

'Je n'ai envie que de t'aimer'. To be sung in one single curve, one single impulse.

'Figure de force' is equally a song to make one *hear* the kind of silence that is the opening of 'Nous avons fait la nuit'.

I was deeply moved when I wrote this song, and I hope that this will be apparent. The pianistic *coda* is essential. Play it in strict time without hurrying (to make sure of applause for the singer).

The last bars look back to 'Bonne journée'. It is very

Il est bien difficile de faire comprendre aux interprètes que le *calme* dans un poème d'amour peut *seul* donner de l'intensité.

Tout le reste est baisers de nourrice.

☯

28 *novembre 1939*

Je relis ce début. Crainte de paraître immodeste par souci de précision. Il est vrai que ce journal n'est pas destiné à être *lu*, mais simplement *consulté*.

☯

2 *décembre 1939*

TROIS POÈMES
DE LOUISE DE VILMORIN

Peu d'êtres m'émeuvent autant que Louise de Vilmorin: parce qu'elle est belle, parce qu'elle boite, parce qu'elle écrit un français d'une pureté innée, parce que son nom évoque des fleurs et des légumes, parce qu'elle aime d'amour ses frères et fraternellement ses amants. Son beau visage fait penser au XVIIe siècle, comme le bruit de son nom. Je l'imagine amie de « Madame » ou peinte par Ph. de Champaigne, en abbesse, un chapelet dans ses longues mains.

Louise échappe toujours à l'enfantillage en dépit de sa maison de campagne où l'on joue autour des pelouses.

L'amour, le désir, le plaisir, la maladie, l'exil, la gêne, sont à la source de son authenticité.

Quelle joie pour moi lorsqu'un jour chez Marie-Blanche de Polignac j'ai lu le poème « Aux officiers de la Garde Blanche » que cette dernière venait de recevoir pour Noël.

J'ai besoin de croire aux mots que j'entends chanter. J'avoue que lorsqu'une dame (bien intentionée, je n'en doute pas) attaque « *j'aime tes yeux, j'aime ta bouche . . . O ma rebelle, ô ma farouche* » . . . en dépit de la musique de Fauré, je ne suis pas convaincu par crainte de l'être trop. Les poèmes de Louise de Vilmorin donnent matière à de véritables mélodies féminines.

difficult to make interpreters understand that *calmness* in a love poem can *alone* give intensity.

All the rest is nothing more than a nurse's kisses.

November 28th, 1939

I read through this opening again. I am afraid of seeming immodest through my anxiety for precision. In truth this diary is not meant to be *read*, but only *consulted*.

December 2nd, 1939

TROIS POÈMES DE LOUISE DE VILMORIN
[THREE POEMS BY LOUISE DE VILMORIN]

Few people move me as much as Louise de Vilmorin:★ because she is beautiful, because she is lame, because she writes French of an innate purity, because her name evokes flowers and vegetables, because she loves her brothers like a lover and her lovers like a sister. Her beautiful face recalls the seventeenth century, as does the sound of her name. I can imagine her as a friend of "Madame", or painted by Ph. de Champaigne,[33] as an abbess, a rosary in her long hands.

Louise always escapes childishness despite her country house where they play on the lawns.

Love, desire, joy, illness, exile, financial difficulties, were at the root of her genuineness.

What a joy for me when one day at the home of Marie-Blanche de Polignac[34] I read the poem 'Aux officiers de la Garde Blanche' which Marie-Blanche had just received for Christmas.

I need to believe in the words that I hear sung. I admit that when a lady (with the best intentions no doubt) begins "J'aime tes yeux, j'aime ta bouche . . . O ma rebelle, O ma farouche" [I love your eyes, I love your mouth . . . O my rebellious one, O my shy one][35] . . . in spite of Fauré's music, I

C'est ce qui m'enchante. Aimant grouper en général plusieurs mélodies je réclamai à Louise d'autres poèmes. Durant l'été de 1937 elle écrivit, pour moi, LE GARÇON DE LIÈGE et EAU DE VIE AU DELÀ.

Le manuscrit du GARÇON DE LIÈGE comprend un quatrain de plus que j'ai supprimé. Louise m'approuva et adopta cette version lorsqu'elle publia ce poème en librairie.

Je regrette, par contre, que dans son recueil *Fiançailles pour rire* elle ait cru bon d'édulcorer l'érotisme voilé d'EAU DE VIE AU DELÀ.

Pour rien au monde je n'apporterais ce changement dans ma version musicale car cela créerait un véritable contresens. La palpitation de l'accompagnement n'aurait plus sa raison d'être.

LE GARÇON DE LIÈGE doit se jouer *vertigineusement* vite.

Le mouvement de métronome, *empirique*, est destiné à sauvegarder l'atmosphère tourbillonnante de la mélodie et à faire valoir la chute du poème. La partie de chant n'est d'ailleurs pas d'un débit précipité, comme celle de piano.

Il faut chanter EAU DE VIE AU DELÀ très légèrement, très simplement, sans rien souligner et cependant sans rien dissimuler.

Les triolets en *staccato* du piano doivent passer au second plan tout en restant précis.

C'est après beaucoup de réflexion que j'ai adopté l'écriture pianistique d'AUX OFFICIERS DE LA GARDE BLANCHE. « Quelle pauvreté » s'écriera le grincheux de Genève en découvrant l'immuable unisson du début. Il m'a donné cependant bien du mal. Quelle tentation d'écrire une harmonie, dès la quatrième mesure et pourtant je suis certain qu'il fallait résister à cette fausse richesse. J'y vois pour ma part plus d'humilité que de misère. Ces doubles croches répétées évoquent la guitare que Louise promène avec elle en allant dîner chez ses amis.

Tout est *préambule* jusqu'à la première invocation: « Officiers de la garde blanche. »

Beaucoup hésité à écrire la modulation en dos d'âne qui souligne « *sur son astre orné de buis, lorsque plus tard je planerai transparent* » de peur qu'on prenne *lorsque plus tard*

am not convinced, for fear of being too convinced. The poems of Louise de Vilmorin provide material for truly feminine songs. That is what delights me. Liking as a rule to group several songs together, I begged Louise for some more poems. During the summer of 1937 she wrote for me 'Le Garçon de Liège' and 'Eau de vie au delà'.

The manuscript of 'Le Garçon de Liège' has one more verse which I did not use. Louise agreed with me about this and adopted this version when the poem was published.

I regret, on the other hand, that in her collection *Fiançailles pour rire* she has thought fit to tone down the veiled eroticism of 'Eau de vie au delà'. Not for the world would I make this alteration in my musical version for that would make nonsense of it. The palpitation in the accompaniment would no longer have any point.

'Le Garçon de Liège' must be played at a dizzy speed. The *empirical* tempo of the metronomic indication is meant to safeguard the turbulent atmosphere of the song and to show to advantage the cadence of the poem. Besides, the writing for the voice requires a much less rapid delivery than that for the piano.

'Eau de vie au delà' should be sung very lightly, very simply, without emphasizing anything, but at the same time without hiding its true meaning. The *staccato* triplets of the piano part must remain in the background while still being precise.

It was after much reflection that I adopted the style of pianistic writing for 'Aux officiers de la Garde Blanche'. "What poor stuff," the grouser[28] of Geneva will exclaim on discovering the unchanging unison of the opening. All the same, it has given me a great deal of trouble. What a temptation to harmonize after the fourth bar and yet I am convinced that this false richness had to be resisted. For my part I see more humility than misery in it. Those repeated semiquavers evoke the guitar that Louise used to take with her when she went to dine with friends.

All is *prelude* until the first invocation: "Officiers de la garde

pour un début de phrase. A la réflexion j'estime ma solution plausible, je ne dis pas qu'il n'en est pas de meilleure. Cette dernière mélodie, doit être « très chantée ».

Je préfère une jolie voix bête à la chanteuse pseudo-intelligente, presque toujours aphone.

❧❧

Les cinq mélodies dont je vais parler maintenant ont été composées pour les récitals Bernac–Poulenc de l'hiver 38–39. Je les nommerai dans l'ordre du programme qui est celui prévu par moi tandis que je les écrivais.

LE JARDIN D'ANNA

A l'époque où j'ai composé les QUATRE POÈMES D'APOL-LINAIRE celui-ci devait faire partie du cycle. Je trouvai im-médiatement la conclusion lyrique et les quelques mesures espagnoles. Le reste bouda. Comme dans tous les poèmes où il s'agit d'énumération d'images, un *tempo* continu et strict est obligatoire. C'est ce que je n'avais pas compris en 1931. J'avais mis ce poème de côté en me jurant bien d'y revenir un jour.

Je l'ai repris sans penser à rien, ce qui était indispensable pour ne pas buter aux mêmes obstacles. Malgré mon huitième de sang alsacien (mon arrière-grand-père paternel était de Colmar) je n'ai nullement pensé à l'Alsace, suggérée ici, en écrivant le JARDIN D'ANNA. Les derniers vers évoquent au contraire, pour moi, une fin de journée de septembre, quelque part en Seine-et-Marne, du côté de Chartrette, avec vue sur le

40

blanche".

I was hesitant about writing the ridge-like modulation which stresses "*sur son astre orné de buis, lorsque plus tard je planerai transparent*" for fear that *lorsque plus tard* could be taken as the beginning of a phrase. On reflection I consider my solution plausible; I do not say it is the best one. This last song must be "very much sung".

I prefer a pretty voice without brains to the pseudo-intelligent singer, usually without voice.

The five songs about which I am going to speak now were composed for the Bernac–Poulenc recitals of the winter 1938/39. I will name them in the order of the programme, which was the order envisaged while I was writing them.

LE JARDIN D'ANNA
[ANNA'S GARDEN]

During the period when I composed the *Quatre Poèmes d'Apollinaire* this song should have been part of the cycle. The lyrical conclusion and the few Spanish bars came to me at once. The rest would not come. As in all poems that concern an enumeration of mental images, a *tempo* that is continuous and strict is essential. It is this that I had not understood in 1931. I had put this poem on one side vowing to return to it one day.

I took it up again with my mind a blank, which is imperative in order to avoid stumbling over the same obstacles as before. In spite of my eighth part of Alsatian blood (my paternal great-grandfather came from Colmar) I did not once think of Alsace while writing 'Le Jardin d'Anna'. On the contrary the last lines evoke for me the end of a September day somewhere in Seine-et-Marne, towards Chartrette, with a view of the

fleuve et la forêt de Fontainebleau.

Débiter toute la mélodie d'un trait, dans un *tempo* continu, pour sauter à pieds joints dans l'érotisme ironique puis la calme volupté de la conclusion.

ALLONS PLUS VITE

Il y a peu de poèmes que j'aie « désirés » plus intensément et plus longtemps. Dès 1935 j'avais fait une esquisse, brûlée depuis et, Dieu merci, totalement oubliée.

Trouvé tout à coup en 1938 la mesure « sur le Boulevard de Grenelle ». Il est rare que je commence une mélodie par le commencement. Un ou deux vers, pris au hasard, m'accrochent et bien souvent me donnent le ton, le rythme secret, la clef de l'œuvre.

Le poème d'Apollinaire débute comme du Baudelaire: « Et le soir vient et les lys meurent » puis, brusquement, après l'envol de quelques vers nobles, atterrit sur un trottoir parisien. J'ai jalousement réservé, après un début en la mineur, le ton de la majeur pour éclairer cet effet de surprise.

J'ai tant traîné la nuit dans Paris que je crois savoir mieux qu'un autre musicien, à quel rythme glisse une pantoufle sur l'asphalte, un soir de mai.

Si l'on ne comprend pas la mélancolie sexuelle du poème il est inutile de chanter cette mélodie.

Pour Apollinaire et pour moi le Boulevard de Grenelle est aussi rare et poétique que le sont, pour d'autres, les bords du Gange.

A vrai dire ce n'est pas exactement au Boulevard de Grenelle que j'ai songé, en écrivant ma musique, mais à son frère jumeau le Boulevard de la Chapelle où j'ai dévalé tant de soirs, lorsque j'habitais Montmartre.

J'ai situé Pauline à la porte de l'Hôtel Molière. On se demande ce que vient faire Molière au pont de chemin de fer de

river and the forest of Fontainebleau.

Maintaining the same *tempo*, launch the whole song in one sweep in order to leap straight into the erotic irony, then the calm voluptuousness of the conclusion.

ALLONS PLUS VITE
[COME ALONG MAKE HASTE]

There are few poems which I "hankered after" more intensely and for longer. As early as 1935 I had made a sketch, subsequently burnt and, thank goodness, totally forgotten. In 1938 the musical phrase for "sur le Boulevard de Grenelle" suddenly came into my mind. I seldom begin a song at the beginning. One or two lines, chosen at random, seize hold of me and very often give me the tone, the secret of the rhythm, the key to the work.

The poem by Apollinaire opens like Baudelaire:[36] "Et le soir vient et les lys meurent" then, abruptly, after taking flight with a few lofty lines, comes to earth on a Parisian pavement. After an opening in A minor I have jealously reserved the major key to illuminate this effect of surprise.

I have so often loitered at night in Paris that I think I know better than any other musician the rhythm of a felt slipper sliding along the pavement on a May evening.

If the sexual melancholy of the poem is not understood it is useless to sing this song.

For Apollinaire and for me the Boulevard de Grenelle is as rare and poetic as the banks of the Ganges are for others. To tell the truth I was not thinking specifically of the Boulevard de Grenelle while I was writing the music, but of its twin brother, the Boulevard de la Chapelle, that I passed through on so many evenings when I lived in Montmartre.

I pictured Pauline at the door of the Hotel Molière. One wonders what Molière[37] was doing on the bridge of the Gare de l'Est. Nevertheless the Hotel exists. Czechoslovakian

l'Est. L'hôtel existe pourtant. On y trouve des prostituées tchécoslovaques en bottes de caoutchouc ciré, pour cent sous . . .

LE PORTRAIT

Depuis des années Colette me promettait des poèmes. Un jour qu'assis auprès de son lit avec Thérèse Dorny et Hélène Jourdan-Morhange je les lui réclamais, « Tenez, prenez cela » me dit-elle en me lançant, en riant, un vaste mouchoir de gaze sur lequel était reproduit, en fac-similé, ce joli poème. Je dois avouer que ma musique traduit bien mal mon admiration pour Colette.

C'est une mélodie quelconque, utile cependant dans le présent groupe car elle amorce, à merveille, qui l'eût cru, TU VOIS LE FEU DU SOIR.

MIROIRS BRÛLANTS

I. TU VOIS LE FEU DU SOIR

Personne ne chantera jamais cette mélodie comme Pierre Bernac. C'est pourquoi je la lui ai dédiée. Je me demande si au « jeu de l'île », ce n'est pas celle de mes mélodies que j'emporterais.

Elle est née de hasards et de rencontres heureuses.

Un matin d'août 1938, juste avant d'aller prendre le train pour Nevers, où Bernac m'attendait pour m'emmener à Anost, j'ai acheté, au bas de chez moi, rue de Médicis, chez Corti, le numéro de *Mesures* qui renfermait ce poème d'Éluard.

Choc merveilleux. C'est au-devant de ce paysage que je

prostitutes are found there in shiny rubber boots, for a hundred sous . . .

LE PORTRAIT
[THE PORTRAIT]

For years Colette had been promising me some poems. One day sitting by her bedside with Thérèse Dorny[38] and Hélène Jourdan-Morhange★, I begged her for some. "Here, take this," she said to me, laughing, as she threw me a very large gauze handkerchief on which this charming poem was reproduced. I must confess that my music expresses very inadequately my admiration for Colette.

It is a very ordinary song, useful nevertheless in the present group for it prepares unbelievably well for 'Tu vois le feu du soir'.

MIROIRS BRÛLANTS
[BURNING MIRRORS]

I. TU VOIS LE FEU DU SOIR
[YOU SEE THE FIRE OF EVENING]

No one will ever sing this song like Pierre Bernac. It is for this reason that I have dedicated it to him. I wonder if among my "desert island discs" this might not be the song of mine I would choose to take with me.

It was born of chance and happy encounters.

One morning in August 1938, just before leaving to take the train for Nevers where Bernac was meeting me in order to drive me to Anost,[39] I bought, below my apartment, at Corti's, in the rue de Médicis, the issue of *Mesures* which included this poem by Éluard.

What a marvellous coincidence! It was to this very country-

45

courais, c'était la vue de ma chambre de travail d'Anost.

Rares sont les endroits où j'ai si bien travaillé, avec tant de légèreté et d'oxygène en moi.

En un peu moins de quatre semaines, en août 1937, j'avais écrit ma messe. Je devais retrouver la même facilité de travail l'année suivante.

Ce n'est pas le hasard qui m'a fait découvrir ce coin du Morvan. Ma nourrice est née et enterrée là-bas. Peu de villes m'émeuvent davantage qu'Autun, peu de montagnes reflètent avec plus de douceur « le feu du soir » que ces monts du Morvan. C'est à la porte de la Bourgogne, avec un air cependant plus léger. La récompense de nos journées de travail c'était d'aller Bernac et moi dîner à Saulieu ou à Arnay-le-Duc.

Si j'ai conçu spontanément TU VOIS LE FEU DU SOIR la réalisation ne m'en a pas moins donné beaucoup de mal. Comme je l'ai déjà écrit, à propos du JARDIN D'ANNA un poème énumératif réclame une cadence immuable. Cette longue mélodie (4 minutes) où il n'y a pas la diversion d'une double croche devait se sauver de la monotonie par le raffinement de l'écriture pianistique et la simplicité de la ligne vocale. J'espère ne pas avoir failli à ce programme. L'arabesque s'élance et se recourbe en deux chutes similaires. Une *coda* d'une page donne à l'ensemble sa portée humaine.

Beaucoup hésité pour la prosodie de « l'été qui la couvre de fruits ». La syllabe *té*, très fermée, à prononcer s'accommode, en général, assez mal d'une note aiguë. Telle est cependant ma première version à laquelle je suis revenu, après bien des tâtonnements, d'accord avec Bernac.

Le pianiste devra jouer toute cette mélodie avec un grand scrupule quant à la stricte valeur des notes. Bien que conçu dans un halo de pédales, cet accompagnement ne doit pas s'en aller à la dérive.

2. JE NOMMERAI TON FRONT

Mélodie ratée. Je la tenais à Anost. Par suite de notre départ

side that I was going; it was the view from the room where I worked at Anost.

Rarely have I worked so well anywhere, with so much lightness and oxygen in me. In a little less than four weeks in August 1937 I had written my Mass.[40] The following year I was to find the same facility in working.

It was not by chance that I discovered this corner of the Morvan. It is there that my nurse was born and is laid to rest. Few towns appeal to me more than Autun, few mountains reflect the "fire of evening" with greater mellowness than the hills of the Morvan. It lies at the approach to Burgundy, yet with a milder atmosphere. To reward ourselves for days of work, Bernac and I would dine at Saulieu or Arnay-le-Duc.[39]

If the conception of 'Tu vois le feu du soir' was spontaneous, the achievement of it none the less gave me a lot of trouble. As I have already written concerning 'Le Jardin d'Anna', an enumerative poem calls for an unchanging flow of movement. This long song (four minutes), where not a single semiquaver disturbs the flow, was to be saved from monotony by the subtlety of the writing for the piano and the simplicity of the vocal line. I hope I have not failed in this project. The arabesque leaps up and rebounds in two similar falls. A *coda* of one page gives to the whole its human significance.

I hesitated a lot over the prosody of "l'été qui la couvre de fruits". The syllable *té*, very closed, is in general rather difficult to pronounce on a high note. This was, however, my first version to which, after many experiments, I returned, in agreement with Bernac.

The pianist must scrupulously observe the strict value of the notes. Although it is conceived in a halo of pedals, the accompaniment must not go adrift from the *tempo*.

2. JE NOMMERAI TON FRONT
[I WILL NAME YOUR BROW][41]

An unsuccessful song. I began it at Anost. After our departure,

anticipé (le père de Bernac se mourant) je ne l'ai reprise que beaucoup plus tard à Noizay. J'avais perdu le fil. Tant pis.

PRIEZ POUR PAIX

Toute ma musique religieuse tourne le dos à mon esthétique parisienne ou banlieusarde. Quand je prie c'est l'Aveyronnais qui reparaît en moi. Evidence de l'hérédité. La foi est puissante chez tous les Poulenc.

Cette prière est influencée par les *Litanies à la Vierge Noire*, ma première œuvre religieuse. Trouvé les vers de Charles d'Orléans dans *Le Figaro* du 28 septembre 38. Me reportant au poème, dans l'édition Garnier, je constate qu'il est beaucoup plus long. Les vers cités me suffisent. Essayé de donner ici une impression de ferveur et surtout d'humilité (pour moi la plus belle qualité de la prière). C'est une prière de sanctuaire de campagne.

Ma conception de la musique religieuse est essentiellement directe et souvent familière.

Respecter dès le début la stricte égalité du *tempo*. Rien ne serait plus malséant que de presser ou de ralentir lorsque la voix attaque.

LA GRENOUILLÈRE

LA GRENOUILLÈRE fait partie des poèmes d'Apollinaire élus depuis longtemps et qui attendent leur tour, des mois, parfois des années. Ici j'ai tâche d'émouvoir d'un bout à l'autre et surtout de ne pas faire rire avec « les femmes à grosse poitrine et bêtes comme choux ».

earlier than we had anticipated (Bernac's father was dying), I did not take it up again until much later at Noizay. I had lost the thread. It can't be helped.

PRIEZ POUR PAIX
[PRAY FOR PEACE]

All my religious music turns its back on the style that is inspired in me by Paris and its outskirts. When I pray it is the native of Aveyron who reawakens in me. This is evidence of heredity. Faith is strong in all the Poulencs.

This prayer is influenced by the *Litanies à la Vierge Noire*,[42] my first religious work. I found the lines of Charles d'Orléans[43] in *Le Figaro* of September 28th, 1938. I looked the poem up in the Garnier edition. I could see that it was far too long. The quoted lines were sufficient for my purpose. I have tried to give here a feeling of fervour and above all of humility (for me the most beautiful quality of prayer). It is a prayer to be spoken in a country church.

My conception of religious music is essentially direct and often intimate.

From the beginning respect the strict regularity of the *tempo*. Nothing could be more unseemly than to hurry or to slow down when the voice enters.

LA GRENOUILLÈRE
[THE FROGGERY]

'La Grenouillère'[44] was one of the poems by Apollinaire which I had chosen long before and which awaited their turn for months, sometimes for years. I have tried to make it touching throughout and above all to cause no amusement with "les femmes à grosse poitrine et bêtes comme choux".

Il n'y a qu'à regarder n'importe quelle photo d'Apollinaire pour comprendre que chez lui l'ironie est toujours voilée de tendresse et de mélancolie.

LA GRENOUILLÈRE évoque un beau passé perdu, des dimanches faciles et heureux.

J'ai pensé, bien entendu, à ces déjeuners de canotiers, peints par Renoir, où les corsages des femmes et les maillots des hommes ont d'autres accords que de couleurs.

Évoqué aussi, avec mon égotisme habituel, les bords de la Marne chers à mon enfance. C'est l'entrechoc de leurs canots qui rythme d'un bout à l'autre cette mélodie tendrement lancinante.

S'abstenir de la chanter si on n'y croit pas, si on introduit des clignements d'yeux et un faux air entendu. Ici il faut être dupe de son cœur. Deux mesures font penser à Moussorgsky. Il serait enfantin de masquer cette influence mais un tel subterfuge me répugnerait.

Je méprise les fils qui rougissent de ressembler à leur père.

CE DOUX PETIT VISAGE

Je tiens beaucoup à cette courte mélodie. La dédicace en fait foi. Raymonde Linossier était le meilleur conseiller de ma jeune musique. Que de fois, depuis des années qu'elle est morte, j'eusse aimé savoir ce qu'elle aurait pensé de telle ou telle de mes œuvres.

Ai tâché de traduire ici, musicalement, toute la tendresse du poème d'Éluard. Je crois avoir réussi spécialement la prosodie de la longue phrase: « A la sortie de l'hiver », chargée d'incidentes vétilleuses.

Il y a dans cette mélodie, à diverses reprises, un doigté qui m'est habituel.

It only needs a glance at any photo of Apollinaire to understand that with him irony is always veiled with tenderness and melancholy.

'La Grenouillère' evokes a beautiful, lost past, Sundays of ease and contentment.

I certainly had in mind those boatmen's lunches, as painted by Renoir, where the bodices of the women and the rowing vests of the men harmonize, and not only in terms of colour.

With my usual egotism, it also evokes the banks of the Marne so dear to my childhood. It is the bumping together of the boats that motivates the rhythm from beginning to end of this tenderly affecting song.

Do not sing it if you do not believe in it, if you are going to introduce winks and a false knowing air. You must be the dupe of your heart. Two bars recall Mussorgsky. It would be childish to hide this influence; such a subterfuge would be repugnant to me.

I despise sons who blush at resembling their fathers.

CE DOUX PETIT VISAGE
[THIS SWEET LITTLE FACE]

I have a great liking for this short song. The dedication bears witness to that. Raymonde Linossier[45] was my best adviser for the music of my youth. How many times during the years since her death would I have liked to have had her opinion on one or the other of my works.

I have tried here to transfuse musically all the tenderness of Éluard's poem. I think I have succeeded, particularly over the prosody of the long phrase: "A la sortie de l'hiver", full of ticklish difficulties.

At various times in this song, there is a fingering which I generally use.

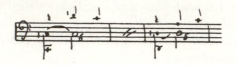

Il faut le respecter car il équilibre solidement la basse de l'harmonie.

Il est bon de ne pas trop se fier au prolongement de son des pédales.

A ce propos, ai-je déjà écrit quelque part combien le jeu des pédales tient une place capitale dans ma musique? Auric riait, jadis, d'une faute sur une de mes épreuves. Le graveur avait écrit « beaucoup de pédales », avec un *s* comme s'il y en avait au moins une douzaine. Au figuré la chose ne serait pas si bête.

Que de couleurs diverses on peut obtenir du jeu des pédales, surtout avec les pianos modernes. C'était le secret de Gieseking qui les employait, à la fois, avec économie et profusion.

Je voudrais persuader les interprètes qu'il est beaucoup plus difficile d'apprendre les *nuances* que les *notes* d'une œuvre. Ce qui me fait dire qu'un orchestre n'est pas au point, ce n'est pas le nombre de fautes commises mais par l'absence de dosage.

Si j'avais composé ma musique sur un Erard de 1830, nul doute qu'elle eût été très différente. Un compositeur se laisse influencer par le bruit de son piano. Du moins je le crois fermement. Debussy composait sur un Bechstein gras et onctueux, Ravel sur un vieil Erard, sec comme une guitare.

J'ai entendu Stravinsky « chercher » sur son Pleyel telle ou telle sonorité de l'orchestration des *Noces*. Je ne les ai jamais retrouvées pareilles sur d'autres pianos et pourtant j'ai joué le IV° piano des *Noces* plus de quarante fois.

Evidemment tout ceci est de peu d'importance et si la qualité d'une œuvre en dépendait, où irions-nous?

Je tiens cependant à redire, une fois encore, que ma musique réclame l'emploi presque constant de la pédale. C'est ce qui

It should be followed because it gives a firm balance to the harmonic bass.

It is wise not to rely too much on the prolongation of the sound by the pedals.

Regarding this, have I already written somewhere that the use of the pedals holds a position of cardinal importance in my music? How Auric had laughed at a fault in one of my proofs. The engraver had written "a great deal of pedals" with an *s* as though there were at least a dozen. Figuratively speaking, this would not be all that stupid.

How many different colours can be found through the use of the pedals, above all with modern pianos. This was the secret of Gieseking,★ who used them with both economy and profusion.

I would like to persuade interpreters that it is much more difficult to learn the *nuances* than the *notes* of a work. If I find an orchestra unsatisfying it is not because of the number of faults they commit but the absence of balance and proportion.

If I had composed my music on an 1830 Erard no doubt it would have been very different. A composer is influenced by the sound of his piano. At least this is my firm belief. Debussy composed on a Bechstein, rich and creamy, Ravel on an old Erard, dry as a guitar.

I have heard Stravinsky★ "seeking" on his Pleyel this or that sonority for *Les Noces*.[13] I have never found similar sonorities again on other pianos and yet I have played the fourth piano in *Les Noces* more than forty times.

Obviously all this is of little importance, and if the quality of a work depended on it, where should we be?

All the same, I must insist once more that my work calls for

estompe la *rigueur* de certaines de mes batteries ou de mes arpèges.

FIANÇAILLES POUR RIRE

Sans la guerre je n'eusse sans doute jamais écrit ce cycle. J'ai hâte de m'expliquer pour me faire pardonner ce que, de prime abord, cette assertion peut avoir de paradoxal. J'ai composé FIANÇAILLES POUR RIRE pour penser mieux à Louise de Vilmorin, enfermée dans son château de Hongrie en 1940, pour Dieu sait combien de temps. Voilà tout le rapport de mon œuvre avec cette horrible tornade. Il est fortuit, comme on voit.

LA DAME D'ANDRÉ doit se chanter très simplement. Auric me reproche le dernier accord qu'il trouve faussement étrange pour une mélodie si simple. Je crois qu'il a tort. L'équivoque tonale empêche la mélodie de conclure et amorce le reste, ce n'est pas ici un artifice.

DANS L'HERBE. Mélodie sans histoire, à chanter très intensément.

IL VOLE. Une de mes mélodies les plus difficiles. Il me semble impossible de l'interpréter sans un sérieux travail et de nombreuses répétitions.

MON CADAVRE. A chanter très simplement, l'archet bien à la corde.

VIOLON. Composé en pensant à un restaurant hongrois des Champs-Elysées où le mari de Louise, le comte Palfi avait fait venir des Tziganes de Budapest. Je n'ai cherché que de très loin à évoquer la couleur locale car c'est une main française qui a écrit le poème. Le musicien transpose également, dans une atmosphère de chez nous, ce rythme du Danube.

VIOLON évoque Paris et son écouteuse au chapeau de Reboux, comme le fox-trott de *L'Enfant et les sortilèges* de Ravel sent son Casino de Paris, sa rue de Clichy, sa rue d'Athènes, où habitait Ravel.

the almost constant use of the pedals. This softens the *severity* of certain of my broken chords or of my arpeggios.

FIANÇAILLES POUR RIRE
[WHIMSICAL BETROTHAL]

Had it not been for the war I should doubtless never have written this cycle. I hasten to excuse myself for an assertion which at first glance may seem paradoxical. I composed *Fiançailles pour rire* so that I could more often turn my thoughts towards Louise de Vilmorin, imprisoned in her castle in Hungary for God knows how long. That was the only connection between my work and this horrible tornado. It is fortuitous, as can be seen.

'La Dame d'André' should be sung very simply. Auric disagrees with the final chord which he finds strange for such a simple song. I think he is wrong. The tonal ambiguity prevents the song from coming to a conclusion and so prepares the way for the following songs; here it is not a trick.

'Dans l'herbe'. Nothing to say about this song. Sing it with great intensity.

'Il vole'. One of the most difficult of my songs. It seems to me impossible to interpret it without serious work and numerous rehearsals.

'Mon cadavre'. To be sung very simply, with a good *legato* tone.

'Violon'. Composed with a Hungarian restaurant in the Champs-Elysées in mind, for which Louise's husband, Count Palffy, had engaged a Hungarian gypsy band from Budapest. I have tried to suggest only very distantly the local colour because the hand that wrote the poem is French. The musician similarly transposes this rhythm of the Danube into our own atmosphere.

'Violon' evokes Paris, and its listener in a hat from Reboux, just as the fox-trot from Ravel's *L'Enfant et les sortilèges* is

FLEURS. Quand on chantera cette mélodie séparément il faudra toujours tâcher de la faire précéder d'une mélodie dans un ton éloigné (VIOLON si possible) ou une mélodie en *la*, ceci afin de sauvegarder cette impression de *ton qui vient de loin*.

Attaqué de plain-pied le ton de ré bémol devient plat. Je crois qu'il y a dans cette mélodie une mélancolie si irrémédiable que l'auditeur lui assigne, dès les premières mesures, son rôle de coda.

Il faut la chanter *humblement*, le lyrisme venant de l'intérieur.

BLEUET

Je ne me suis pas mis dans une posture héroïque en écrivant cette mélodie. Cela ne m'irait d'ailleurs pas car je n'ai rien d'un barde. Ému simplement au plus profond de moi-même, par la résonance si humaine du poème d'Apollinaire. L'humilité, qu'il s'agisse de la prière ou du sacrifice d'une vie, c'est ce qui me touche le plus.

> « *Il est dix-sept heures et tu saurais mourir*
> *Sinon mieux que tes aînés*
> *du moins plus pieusement* »

Telle est pour moi la clef du poème, l'éclairage exact du drame.

Nous sommes loin de « Ceux qui pieusement sont morts » avec grand renfort de clairons, de marbre, de lampadaires crêpés, de drapeaux. Pour cela même nous touchons de plus près, je crois, à cet instant mystérieux où, laissant sa dépouille au vestiaire, l'âme s'envole après un long regard jeté sur « la douceur d'autrefois ».

redolent of the Casino de Paris,[46] the rue de Clichy, the rue d'Athènes where Ravel lived.

'Fleurs'. Whenever this song is sung separately always try to precede it with a song in a distant key ('Violon' if possible), or a song in A; this will safeguard the impression of a *sound that comes from far away*.

If it is begun without this preparation of key, D flat sounds dull. I believe that there is such melancholy here that after the first bars the listener will assign to the song its role of *coda*.

It should be sung with *humility*, the lyricism coming from within.

⊚⊚

BLEUET
[YOUNG SOLDIER]

I didn't adopt a heroic stance when writing this song. That would, moreover, not have suited me, because there is nothing of the bard about me. I was quite simply moved to the depths of my being by the intensely human overtones of Apollinaire's poem. Humility, whether it concerns prayer or the sacrifice of a life, is what touches me most.

> It is five o'clock and you would know how to die
> if not better than your elders
> at least with more piety

That is for me the key to the poem, the perfect clarification of the drama.

We are far from "Those who have died piously" with pealing sounds from the organ, with marble, with draped candelabra, with flags. It is more befitting, I believe, for that mysterious moment when leaving the mortal remains in the vestiary, the soul flies away after a long, last look at "la

57

Tout ceci pour prouver combien ce serait un contresens de chanter BLEUET *pompeusement. Intimement* c'est peut-être ce que j'aurais dû marquer comme nuance initiale.

☙❧

Août 1932

LE BAL MASQUÉ

Un jour qu'à Noizay j'étais de mauvaise humeur, Jacques Février me conseilla de jouer le BAL MASQUÉ en me disant « Tu verras, je te connais, cela ira mieux après ».

Comme le cher garçon avait raison. C'est vrai, le BAL MASQUÉ me désarme. J'ai pour lui toutes les indulgences. Je suis certain qu'on n'aime pas véritablement ma musique si on le méconnaît. C'est du Poulenc cent pour cent. A une dame du Kamtchatka qui m'écrirait pour me demander comment je suis fait, je lui enverrais mon portrait au piano par Cocteau, mon portrait par Bérard, le BAL MASQUÉ et les *Motets pour un temps de Pénitence.* Je crois qu'elle se ferait ainsi une idée très exacte de Poulenc–Janus.

Le BAL MASQUÉ a été composé pour un « spectacle concert » organisé en 1932 au théâtre d'Hyères par mes amis Charles de Noailles.

J'avais écrit pour eux en 1929, *Aubade,* dans la mélancolie et l'angoisse. Je voulais cette fois prendre une joyeuse revanche.

Dès l'automne 31, j'établis le plan de cette cantate profane. Je n'avais que l'embarras du choix dans toute l'œuvre bouffonne de Max Jacob.

Depuis longtemps « le comte d'Artois qui fait, sur un toit, son compte d'ardoises » me clignait de l'œil et le « réparateur perclus de vieux automobiles » me fascinait. J'adoptais le premier pour l'air de bravoure et le dernier pour le finale.

douceur d'autrefois" ["the sweetness of former days"].

All this proves what a misconception it would be to sing 'Bleuet' *grandiloquently*. *Intimately* should perhaps have been my marking for the initial expression.

∞

August 1932

LE BAL MASQUÉ
[THE MASKED BALL]

One day at Noizay, I was in a bad mood. Jacques Février★ advised me to play *Le Bal masqué*, saying: "You will see, I know you, you will feel better afterwards".

How right the dear fellow was. It is true, the *Bal masqué* disarms me. I feel very indulgent towards it. I am sure that no one who belittles it can truly like my music. It is a hundred per cent Poulenc. To a lady in Kamchatka[47] who would write to ask me what I am like, I would send my portrait at the piano by Cocteau,★ my portrait by Bérard,[48] *Le Bal masqué* and the *Motets pour un temps de pénitence.*[42] I believe she would then have a very clear idea of Poulenc–Janus.

Le Bal masqué was composed for a "musical entertainment" organized in 1932 at the theatre in Hyères by my friends the Noailles.[49]

In 1929 I had written *Aubade* for them, in melancholy and anguish. This time I wanted to make up for this by writing joyously.

Since the autumn of '31 I had been working out the design of this secular cantata. There was almost too much choice among all the farcical works of Max Jacob.

For a long time "le comte d'Artois qui fait, sur un toit, son compte d'ardoises" had been beckoning to me and the "réparateur perclus de vieux automobiles" had fascinated me. I used the former for the bravura aria and the latter for the finale.

MALVINA et LA DAME AVEUGLE, qui complètent la partie vocale, sont peintes d'après nature.

La première « se tirebouchonne comme une valse tzigane », minaude, joue à la Duchesse, le petit doigt en l'air, va au bal en bas bleus, ce qui lui est fatal: on lui parle de Nietzsche alors qu'elle souhaitait tout simplement être prise à la hussarde.

Qui de nous n'a connu de telles prétentieuses, victimes de leurs concepts.

J'ai beaucoup pensé en écrivant LA DAME AVEUGLE à une étonnante grosse rentière qui hantait, aux environs de 1912, l'île de Beauté à Nogent-sur-Marne.

Elle habitait un chalet mi-suisse, mi-normand et passait ses journées à faire des réussites assise sur son perron, vêtue d'une robe de soie noire. Dans un fauteuil de rotin, à quelques pas d'elle, une manière de Landru, avec binocle, casquette de cycliste, lisait son journal.

En découvrant dans *Laboratoire Central* le poème de Max Jacob, j'ai eu absolument l'impression de retrouver une vieille photo dans un album de campagne.

En écrivant LE BAL MASQUÉ je parlais donc de choses que je connaissais.

Il fallait maintenant trouver une optique spéciale pour faire passer la rampe à tout ce carnaval.

C'est la seule de mes œuvres où je pense avoir trouvé le moyen de magnifier une atmosphère banlieusarde qui m'est chère. Ceci grâce aux mots de Max pleins de ricochets imprévus et à la matière instrumentale que j'ai employée.

Ici la *couleur* souligne l'emphatique, le ridicule, le pitoyable, le terrifiant. C'est l'atmosphère des crimes en chromo du *Petit Parisien* des dimanches de mon enfance.

« Quelle horreur! » s'écriait à cette époque la cuisinière de la grand-mère. « *Encore* un type qui a assassiné sa belle-sœur ». Il se pourrait que la DAME AVEUGLE ait subi le même sort.

J'ai cru pendant longtemps que LE BAL MASQUÉ ne franchirait pas les frontières jusqu'au jour où le public de Genève, en trépignant, a hurlé « bis » pour le finale. Je suis certain maintenant que plus une œuvre est authentiquement nationale

'Malvina' and 'La dame aveugle', which complete the vocal part, are painted from life.

The first "se tirebouchonne comme une valse tzigane" [twists into spirals like a Hungarian gypsy waltz], simpers, plays the Duchess, her little finger raised, goes to the ball in blue stockings — which is fatal for her: they talk to her about Nietzsche[50] when all she wants is to be taken by storm.

Who among us have not known pretentious creatures like this, victims of their own imaginings.

While writing 'La dame aveugle' I often recalled an astonishingly stout lady of apparently independent means who, around 1912, frequented the Île de Beauté at Nogent-sur-Marne.

She lived in a chalet, half Swiss, half Norman and passed her days playing patience, sitting on her front door steps attired in a dress of black silk. On a cane armchair a few steps from her sat a man who looked like Landru,[51] with pince-nez and a cyclist's cap, reading his newspaper.

In discovering in *Laboratoire Central* the poem by Max Jacob, I had the definite impression of having found again an old photo in a country album. In writing *Le Bal masqué* I was speaking of things that were familiar to me.

It was necessary now to find a special perspective to get all this carnival over to the listener.

It is the only one among my works where I think I have found the means of heightening that atmosphere of the environs of Paris which is so dear to me. This is thanks to Max's words full of unforeseen ricochets, and the instrumental material that I have used.

Here the *colour* underlines the bombast, the ridiculous, the pitiable, the terrifying. It is the atmosphere of the colour prints of crimes in the *Petit Parisien* of the Sundays of my childhood.

"How horrible!" cried my grandmother's cook at this time. "*Once again* a chap has murdered his sister-in-law." It could be that the 'Dame aveugle' had suffered the same fate.

For a long time I believed that *Le Bal masqué* would not get

plus elle touche l'étranger. Le public, bien entendu ne saisit pas toutes les nuances, mais perçoit, dans l'ensemble, la valeur ethnique de l'œuvre.

Pour l'interprétation du BAL je redirai ce que j'ai tant de fois écrit au cours de ce journal: le chanteur doit *croire* avant tout aux mots qu'il débite. Pas de réticences, pas de faux airs entendus, pas de clins d'œil complices.

Gilbert Moryn qui a créé cette œuvre y était de premier ordre. Il n'aurait pas chanté Scarpia avec plus de conviction et plus de sérieux.

Le *finale* doit être ahurissant et presque terrifiant. C'est la clef de l'œuvre et, pour moi, un portrait exact de Max Jacob par lui-même, tel que je l'ai connu lorsqu'il habitait la rue Gabrielle à Montmartre en 1920. La partie de piano du BAL est capitale. Il faut la jouer en virtuose avec une palette très variée. Mettre la pédale abondamment mais avec beaucoup de soin. Les rythmes, lents ou vifs, sont *implacables*. Au bout des vingt minutes que dure LE BAL MASQUÉ le public doit être stupéfait et diverti comme les gens qui descendent d'un manège de la Foire du Trône.

TORÉADOR
(Chanson hispano-italienne)

Bernac prétend que je chante cette mélodie, pardon cette chanson, comme personne.

C'est dire assez que la voix ne compte pas pour l'interprétation de cette plaisanterie musicale et que les « oins oins » qui sortent de mon nez, qui n'est pas grec, suffisent pour divertir les personnes auxquelles je la destine.

Le texte de Jean Cocteau a été écrit en 1917. Pierre Bertin, à cette époque, aidé par un groupe de musiciens, d'écrivains et

across to the public, until the day when the audience at Geneva stamped and shouted "encore" at the end. I now feel certain that the more truly national a work is, the more it appeals to the foreigner. The public will not, of course, understand all the subtleties, but they will appreciate the national significance of the work as a whole.

For the interpretation of *Le Bal* I will repeat what I have written so many times in the course of this Diary: the singer must above all believe in the words that he sings. No reticence, no false knowing looks, no conniving winks.

Gilbert Moryn,★ who created this work, was first class. He would not have sung Scarpia[52] with more conviction and more seriousness.

The *finale* must be flabbergasting and almost terrifying. It is the key to the work and, for me, it is an exact portrait of Max Jacob by himself, just as I knew him when he lived in the rue Gabrielle in Montmartre in 1920.

The piano part of *Le Bal* is of great importance. It must be played with virtuosity and with a very varied palette. Use the pedal plentifully but with great care. The rhythms, slow or brisk, are *implacable*. At the end of *Le Bal masqué*, which lasts twenty minutes, the public should be stupefied and exhilarated like people who get off a merry-go-round at the Foire du Trône.[53]

TORÉADOR
[A SPANISH–ITALIAN SONG]

Bernac maintains that I sing this mélodie, forgive me, this *song*,[54] like nobody else.

It is enough to say that the voice does not matter for the interpretation of this musical pleasantry and that the "oins oins" coming from my nose, which is not Grecian, are sufficient to amuse the people for whom it is destined.

The text, by Jean Cocteau, was written in 1917. Pierre Bertin,★ at this time, aided by a group of musicians, writers

de peintres (Satie, Auric, Honegger, moi-même, Cocteau, Max Jacob, Cendrars, La Fresnaye, Kisling, Derain, Fauconnet) voulut donner aux Vieux Colombier une soirée de spectacles-concerts dans un style Bobino supérieur. Ce projet n'eut pas de lendemain. Disons tout de suite que c'était le début de cette confusion des genres qui, hélas, ne s'est que trop longtemps prolongée.

Chacun à sa place, c'est ce que devraient se répéter sans cesse les artistes soucieux de leur standing.

TORÉADOR, je dois l'avouer, appartient à ce genre hybride. Une Marie Dubas qui fait trépigner la salle de l'Empire avec Pedro endosserait, j'en suis certain, une belle veste en présentant à ce même public TORÉADOR.

TORÉADOR, caricature de la chanson de music-hall, ne peut donc s'adresser qu'à une élite restreinte.

C'est exactement le type de la chanson pour faire rire, autour d'un piano, quelques amis à la page. Je ne donne pas longtemps pour que le cabaret littéraire devienne intolérable comme tous les genres faux.

Ceci dit, j'aime beaucoup TORÉADOR. Longtemps inédit, je me suis décidé à le publier aux environs de 1932 sur le conseil de mon cher vieil ami Jacques-Emile Blanche.

Ce parrainage en dit long sur le côté littéraire de l'œuvre et sur le public auquel on peut prétendre.

Octobre 40

BANALITÉS

Encore une fois c'est à Guillaume Apollinaire que j'ai fait appel pour ce cycle.

Depuis longtemps j'avais élu SANGLOTS et les curieuses FAGNES DE WALLONIE. J'ai déjà noté ici ma manie de mettre de côté, par avance, des poèmes.

and painters (Satie, Auric, Honegger,[55] myself, Cocteau, Max Jacob, Cendrars,[56] La Fresnaye, Kisling,[57] Derain,[58] Fauconnet[59]) wanted to give at the Vieux-Colombier[60] an evening of musical entertainment in the style of superior Bobino.[61] This project had no future. Let us say at once that it was the beginning of that confusion of styles which, alas, is only too long-lasting.

Each to his own sphere. Artists concerned about their standing should not cease to repeat this to themselves.

'Toréador', I must confess, belongs to this hybrid style. A certain Marie Dubas★ who, with Pedro, makes the audience stamp its feet at the Empire,[62] would don, I am sure, a fine jacket on presenting 'Toréador' to this same public.

'Toréador', a caricature of a music-hall song, could only appeal to a chosen few. It is exactly the type of song to make a few intimate friends laugh around the piano. I do not give the literary cabaret long before it will become intolerable, as all false genres do.

All the same, I like 'Toréador' very much. Having left it unpublished for a long time, I decided to publish it about 1932 on the advice of my dear old friend, Jacques-Emile Blanche.[63]

This sponsorship says a lot for the literary side of the work and for the public whose support could be relied upon.

October 1940

BANALITÉS
[BANALITIES]

Once again I turned to Guillaume Apollinaire for this cycle.

I had chosen 'Sanglots' and the curious 'Fagnes de wallonie' long before. I have already spoken here of my inveterate habit of putting certain poems aside in advance.

When in October 1940 I had just got back to Noizay, on

Lorsqu'en octobre 1940 j'ai regagné Noizay, en rangeant ma bibliothèque, j'ai feuilleté, une fois de plus, et avec quelle émotion, ces revues littéraires qui de 1914 à 1923 ont enchanté mon adolescence. La série des numéros de *Littérature* a cette fois retenu tout particulièrement mon attention. Ce peut-il que tant de beaux poèmes aient paru, là-dedans, avec un air de n'y pas toucher.

C'est d'ailleurs le privilège, modeste, de ce genre de Revues. Tout à coup, on tombe sur un poème de Valéry, depuis épinglé d'or dans toutes les anthologies.

Dans le cas présent, il ne s'agit, pour Apollinaire, que de délicieux vers de mirliton groupés sous le titre de *Banalités* (Voyage à Paris — Hôtel).

Quand on me connaît, il paraîtra tout naturel que j'aie ouvert une bouche de carpe pour happer les vers délicieusement stupides du VOYAGE À PARIS.

Lorsqu'il s'agit de Paris j'y vais souvent de ma larme ou de ma note.

HÔTEL, c'est encore Paris; une chambre à Montparnasse.

Il ne m'en fallait pas plus pour me décider à entreprendre un cycle dans lequel figureraient SANGLOTS et FAGNES.

Restait à trouver une méthode initiale rythmique, SANGLOTS devant clore la série avec gravité.

C'est alors que je me souviens d'une chanson, assez Maeterlinck, qu'Apollinaire avait insérée dans une étrange et belle prose intitulée *Onirocritique*. Au mois de juin 40, marchant comme trouffion sur la route de Cahors, je m'étais mis à fredonner, je ne sais pas pourquoi « Par les portes d'Orkenise ».

Dans BANALITÉS, je n'en ai pas fait une chanson de route pas plus, d'ailleurs, que je n'ai repensé aux bords du Lot où j'avais trouvé le premier vers.

Rien n'est plus déroutant que le jeu des images, chez moi.

Orkenise, c'est une rue d'Autun conduisant à la Porte romaine. Pour ce qui est de l'interprétation, tout ce que j'ai consigné ici à propos de LA GRENOUILLÈRE est bon pour VOYAGE À PARIS, tout ce que j'ai écrit sur le FEU DU SOIR valable pour SANGLOTS.

going through my library I turned the pages once again — and with how much emotion — of those literary reviews which, from 1914 to 1923, had enchanted my adolescence. This time the series of issues of *Littérature* particularly held my attention. How could it be that so many beautiful poems had appeared there in such modest guise?

But that is the unassuming privilege of this type of review. All at once one comes across a poem by Valéry,[64] now the pride of all the anthologies.

In the present instance, as far as Apollinaire was concerned, I chose only the delicious lines of doggerel grouped under the title *Banalités* ('Voyage à Paris' — 'Hôtel').

To anyone who knows me it will seem quite natural that I should open my mouth like a carp to snap up the deliciously stupid lines of 'Voyage à Paris'.

Anything that concerns Paris I approach with tears in my eyes and my head full of music.

'Hôtel' is again Paris; a room in Montparnasse.

Nothing more was needed to decide me to embark on a cycle in which 'Sanglots' and 'Fagnes' would appear.

It remained to find an opening rhythmical song, since 'Sanglots' would conclude the cycle with gravity. Then I remembered a song, a little Maeterlinck[65] in style, that Apollinaire had inserted in a strange and beautiful prose piece entitled *Onirocritique*. In June 1940, marching as a soldier on the road to Cahors, I began to whistle, I do not know why, 'Par les portes d'Orkenise'.[66]

In *Banalités* I did not make a marching song of it, nor was I recalling the banks of the Lot where the first line had come to my mind. With me nothing is more confusing than the influence of visual impressions.

Orkenise is a road in Autun leading to the Roman gate. As for the interpretation, all that I have suggested here concerning 'La grenouillère' applies to 'Voyage à Paris', all that I have written about 'Le feu du soir' is appropriate for 'Sanglots'.

Avril 45

Je reprends ce Journal par mauvaise humeur. Je l'ai commencé d'ailleurs dans des circonstances analogues. Hier récital de Mme X qui chante avec intelligence, mais avec un minimum de voix. Une pianiste impeccable mais d'une *avarice* sordide quant à la pédale, l'accompagnait.

Il paraît que c'était très bien. Je suis sorti ivre de colère de chez Gaveau.

Je me fous des chanteuses intelligentes. Il me faut *du chant* avec une bonne sauce de pédale (le beurre, quoi!) sans cela ma musique en crève.

Mai 45

Le Festival de mes mélodies (27 avril) m'a rendu malade, avant et après. Pour le premier concert, uniquement consacré à mes œuvres, j'avais choisi un genre dans lequel je pouvais espérer gagner la partie, mais c'est égal, c'est une rude épreuve, un récital de mélodies. A dessein j'avais écarté le *tout cuit* qui n'est généralement pas *le meilleur*, donc, pas d'*airs chantés*.

Désormière m'écrit le 24 mai: « Je me suis beaucoup réjoui du grand succès de ton concert, le retentissement en a été considérable ». Comme Déso n'est pas suspect d'indulgence cette phrase me touche beaucoup et m'encourage. Suzanne Balguerie et Bernac s'étaient d'ailleurs surpassés.

Nombreux articles. F. G. me traite de Puck et prétend que « j'ajoute un postlude à un genre qui a fait son temps . . . »

Je voudrais bien savoir pourquoi cette forme musicale serait périmée. Il me semble que tant qu'il y aura des poètes on pourra écrire des mélodies. Si l'on mettait sur ma tombe: Cigît Francis Poulenc, le musicien d'Apollinaire et d'Éluard, il me semble que ce serait mon plus beau titre de gloire.

April 1945

I am resuming this diary in a bad mood. I began it, moreover, in similar circumstances. Yesterday a recital by Mme X who sings with intelligence but a minimum of voice. The accompanist was impeccable but she was terribly mean when it came to using enough pedal.

It was a success, it seems. I left the Salle Gaveau in a fury.

I detest intelligent singers. I like to hear some *singing* with a good sauce of pedal (the butter!), without which my music is destroyed.

May 1945

The Festival of my songs (27th April) made me ill, both before and afterwards. For the first concert, dedicated solely to my works, I had chosen a type of song which I hoped might make a good impression, but all the same, it is a severe test, a recital of songs. Intentionally, I had avoided the most *popular* which are not as a rule the *best*, hence none of the *airs chantés*.

Désormière★ wrote to me on the 24th May: "I am highly delighted by the great success of your concert, it has created a considerable stir." As Déso could not be suspected of leniency, this phrase touched me deeply and gave me encouragement. Suzanne Balguerie★ and Bernac surpassed themselves.

Numerous reviews. F.G.[67] treated me as a kind of Puck and maintained that "I add a postlude to a form which has had its day . . .".

I should very much like to know why this musical form should be out of date. It seems to me that as long as there are poets there will be songs. If on my tomb could be inscribed: Here lies Francis Poulenc, the musician of Apollinaire and Éluard, I would consider this to be my finest title to fame.

20 juillet 45. Larche

CHANSONS VILLAGEOISES

Écrites en septembre 42, juste après la création des *Animaux Modèles*, les CHANSONS VILLAGEOISES en découlent directement quant à l'orchestration et même au style harmonique. Je les ai conçues comme un tour de chant symphonique pour un *fort* baryton Verdi (Iago).

Les textes de Fombeure évoquent, pour moi, le Morvan où j'ai passé de si merveilleux étés!

C'est par nostalgie des environs d'Autun que j'ai composé ce recueil. Rien de spécial à dire pour l'interprétation que je n'aie déjà écrit ici. (Au sujet des CHANSONS GAILLARDES, du BAL MASQUÉ: pas de clins d'œil. Il faut y aller carrément.)

Dans le Morvan, on se sert de salles de bal démontables avec plancher ciré, rideaux de crochet, banquettes de peluche, lustres de cuivre. Tout cela, dans mon souvenir, sert de cadre aux GARS QUI VONT À LA FÊTE « rasés à la cuiller » et dansent chez Julien le violoneux.

Sur les mots « le piston, la clarinette » un *tutti* d'orchestre me plaît, pour son odeur vulgaire de « lotion du dimanche ».

C'EST LE JOLI PRINTEMPS doit se chanter et se jouer clair et triste comme un jour d'avril.

LE MENDIANT est très influencé par Moussorgski, cela provient *tout naturellement* du sujet.

MÉTAMORPHOSES

Je n'ai pas grand-chose à en dire. Chanter: REINE DES MOUETTES très vite et légèrement, C'EST AINSI QUE TU ES, surtout

July 20th, 1945, Larche

CHANSONS VILLAGEOISES
[VILLAGE SONGS]

Written in September 1942, just after the creation of *Animaux modèles*,[68] the *Chansons villageoises* sprang directly from that work as far as their orchestration is concerned and even in their harmonic style. I conceived them as a symphonic "song turn" for a heavy Verdi baritone (Iago).

The texts by Fombeure[69] evoke for me the Morvan where I have spent such wonderful summers! It is through nostalgia for the surroundings of Autun that I have composed this collection.

Nothing special to say about the interpretation that I have not already written here. (On the subject of the *Chansons gaillardes*, of *Le Bal masqué*: no knowing looks. Sing them quite straightforwardly.)

In the Morvan it is possible to buy portable ballrooms with polished floors, crochet curtains, plush seats, copper candelabras. All that, in my memory, serves as a frame for 'Les gars qui vont à la fête' "rasés à la cuiller" [shaved to the underskin] and dancing at Julien the fiddler's.

On the words "le piston, la clarinette" I like a *tutti* from the orchestra, to stress the common odour of "Sunday after-shave".

'C'est le joli printemps'. The singing and playing of this song must be as clear and sad as an April day.

'Le mendiant' is very much influenced by Mussorgsky, something that sprang *quite naturally* from the subject.

MÉTAMORPHOSES

I have not a great deal to say about these. Sing: 'Reine des mouettes' very fast and lightly, 'C'est ainsi que tu es', above all

sans afféterie.

PAGANINI est une mélodie *tremplin* qui ne finit pas bien un numéro.

෴

DEUX POÈMES D'ARAGON

A la suite du Festival de mes mélodies, F. G. m'a reproché d'avoir transposé le poème d'Aragon dans une atmosphère à la Devéria.

Aurait-il fallu que je prenne la palette de Delacroix pour traduire ces vers, beaucoup plus près de Musset que de Baudelaire? Je crois que c'est moi qui suis dans le vrai. Quand on met en musique un texte, on le pèse tant de fois qu'on en connaît, très vite, la densité exacte.

C'est un poème dont l'extrême mélancolie vient d'une grande finesse de touche:

> *Une chanson du temps passé*
> *Parle d'un chevalier blessé.*

> . . . .

> *De la prairie où vient danser*
> *Une éternelle fiancée . . .*

C'est ravissant, doucement émouvant, mais qu'on songe au ton d'Éluard dans « Figure humaine »:

> *De tous les printemps du monde*
> *Celui-ci est le plus laid*

Je n'ai pas la prétention de résoudre musicalement les

without affectation.

'Paganini' is a *bridging* song[70] which is not a good end to a group.

DEUX POÈMES D'ARAGON
[TWO POEMS BY ARAGON]
('C' and 'Fêtes galantes')

Following the Festival of my songs, F.G. reproached me for having transposed Aragon's[71] poem into the style of Devéria.[72]

Ought I to have taken the palette of Delacroix to set these lines, much closer to Musset[72] than to Baudelaire? I feel that I am in the right. When I set a text to music I consider and appraise it so many times that I know very quickly the exact weight of its meaning.

It is a poem of which the extreme sadness comes from great subtlety of style:

> *Une chanson du temps passé*
> *Parle d'un chevalier blessé*
> . . .
> *De la prairie ou vient danser*
> *Une éternelle fiancée*
>
> [A song of bygone days
> tells of a wounded knight.
> . . .
> of the meadow where comes dancing
> an eternal betrothed . . .]

It is charming, tenderly moving, but consider the tone of Éluard in 'Figure humaine':

> *De tous les printemps du monde*
> *Celui-ci est le plus laid*

problèmes poétiques par l'*intelligence* (les voix du cœur et de l'instinct sont plus sûres) mais on imagine bien qu'avant d'écrire une mélodie je me pose avant tout le problème de la couleur générale.

L'accompagnement de C. est très difficile à cause du jeu des pédales et des batteries de croches à estomper.

Il faut l'interpréter avec poésie, c'est là tout le secret.

On imagine ce qu'un Gieseking aurait pu faire . . .

∽◎∽

MONTPARNASSE — HYDE PARK

J'ai mis quatre ans pour écrire MONTPARNASSE. Je ne regrette pas le soin que j'y ai apporté car c'est probablement une de mes meilleures mélodies.

Plus je relis Apollinaire, plus je suis frappé du rôle poétique de Paris dans son œuvre. C'est pourquoi, dans le tumulte des *Mamelles*, j'ai, par exemple, toujours respecté les oasis de tendresse suscitées par le mot *Seine* ou par le mot *Paris*.

MONTPARNASSE est un merveilleux poème écrit en 1912.

Qu'on songe à ce Montparnasse découvert tout à coup par Picasso, Braque, Modigliani, Apollinaire.

Seul Max Jacob, poète-sacristain, ne voulant pas quitter Montmartre et sa basilique, demeura rue Gabrielle. J'ai trouvé la musique du vers « Un poète lyrique d'Allemagne » à Noizay, en 41.

Toute la fin (depuis « Vous connaissez de son pavé ») à Noizay, en 43.

Les deux premiers vers, en 44, à Paris.

[Of all the springtimes of the world
this is the ugliest]

I have never claimed to resolve poetic problems by means of
the *intellect* (the voices of the heart and of intuition are more
reliable) but it can be well imagined that before writing a song
I consider before all else the problem of the prevailing colour.

The accompaniment of the song 'C' is very difficult owing
to the use of the pedals and the quick succession of quaver
chords which should be veiled.

It should be interpreted poetically, that is the whole secret.

Imagine what a Gieseking would have made of it . . .

MONTPARNASSE — HYDE PARK

It took me four years to write 'Montparnasse'. I have no
regrets for the care I took over it for it is probably one of my
best songs.

The more I re-read Apollinaire the more I am struck by the
poetic role that Paris plays in his work. That is why, for
example, in the tumult of *Les Mamelles*[73] I have always
respected the oasis of tenderness created by the word *Seine* or
by the word *Paris*.

'Montparnasse' is a marvellous poem written in 1912.

Let us imagine this Montparnasse all at once discovered by
Picasso,[74] Braque,[75] Modigliani,[76] Apollinaire.

Max Jacob alone, poet–sacristan, not wanting to leave
Montmartre and its basilica, lived in the rue Gabrielle. The
music for the line "Un poète lyrique d'Allemagne" came to
my mind at Noizay, in 1941.

All the end part (after "Vous connaissez de son pavé") at
Noizay in 1943.

Restaient quelques vers dont la terrible incidente:

Donnez-moi, pour toujours, une chambre à la semaine.

Je l'ai cueillie au vol à Noizay, en 43.

Ensuite j'ai laissé macérer ces fragments et tout mis au point, en trois jours, à Paris en février 45.

Cette méthode de travail, par bonds, pourra surprendre. Elle m'est cependant assez habituelle lorsqu'il s'agit de mélodies. J'ai eu l'occasion de voir des manuscrits de la comtesse de Noailles, elle opérait souvent ainsi, fixant, après des lignes de points de suspension, tel mot, au milieu d'un vers à venir.

Comme *jamais* je ne transpose dans un autre ton, par facilité, la musique que je viens de trouver pour un vers ou même pour quelques mots, il s'ensuit que les raccords sont souvent difficiles et qu'il me faut du recul pour trouver l'endroit exact où, parfois, je dois, sur place, moduler.

J'écrirai de HYDE PARK ce que j'ai écrit de PAGANINI. C'est une mélodie tremplin, rien de plus.

Octobre 1945

Je déteste musicalement ce qu'on appelle l'esprit pince-sans-rire, par exemple certaines mélodies de Roussel comme le « Bachelier de Salamanque » ou « Cœur en péril ».

Très rapidement les bis immanquables que suscitent ces deux pochades s'émousseront, alors que « Fantoches » de Debussy, grâce à sa poésie foncière ne prendra jamais une ride. Le texte de Franc-Nohain pour l'*Heure espagnole* est *caustique* ce qui est bien différent.

Comme le liquide de l'aquafortiste ronge la plaque de

The first two lines, in 1944, in Paris.

Several lines still remained including the terribly difficult:

Donnez-moi, pour toujours, une chambre à la semaine.

This came to me during the flight to Noizay, in 1943.

After this I let these fragments macerate and perfected the whole in three days, in Paris in February 1945.

This way of working in fits and starts may be surprising. Nevertheless it is quite customary with me where songs are concerned. I once had an opportunity to see the manuscripts of the Countess de Noailles[77] who often worked in this way, fixing, after some suspended lines, a certain word in the middle of a line that was to come.

As I *never* transpose music which I have just conceived for a certain line, or even for several words, into another key to make it easier for myself, it follows that the linking up is often difficult and I need to stand back in order to find the exact place where I am at times obliged to modulate.

I will give similar advice for 'Hyde Park' to that which I gave for 'Paganini'. It is a bridging song, nothing more.

October 1945

Musically I detest what is called dry sarcastic wit, for example certain songs by Roussel★ like 'Le Bachelier de Salamanque' or 'Cœur en péril'.

Very quickly the inevitable repeats inherent in these sketches cause them to lose their point, whereas Debussy's 'Fantoches', due to its intrinsic poetry, will never show a wrinkle. Franc-Nohain's text for *L'Heure espagnole* is *caustic*, which is quite different.

As the engraver's liquid etches the copper plate, the words

cuivre, les mots et les harmonies mordent ici profondément en dessinant d'indélébiles arabesques.

Le poème de Guillaume Apollinaire pour les MAMELLES DE TIRÉSIAS, plein d'arrière-plans poétiques ne tombe jamais dans un humour à fleur de peau. C'est ce dont je me suis persuadé, encore hier, en relisant les épreuves de ma partition.

Il faudra donc *chanter*, d'un bout à l'autre, les MAMELLES comme du Verdi. Cela ne sera peut-être pas très facile à faire comprendre aux interprètes qui s'en tiennent généralement à l'apparence des choses.

Janvier 46

Bernac supervisant mes projets de recueil s'est efforcé (comme pour l'élaboration de nos *programmes de concert*) d'apposer chaque mélodie à la suivante, dans l'éclairage le plus favorable. C'est toute la question de « l'accrochage » aussi capitale en musique qu'en peinture.

A ce propos j'ai souvent repensé à l'histoire suivante: la veille du vernissage d'une exposition Manet, à l'Orangerie, voici quelques années, je déjeunais chez mon cher vieil ami J.-Emile Blanche, beaucoup meilleur peintre qu'on le dit, d'une vaste culture et d'un goût parfait. M'ayant proposé de l'accompagner à l'Orangerie pour l'accrochage j'acceptai avec joie. A peine le seuil de l'exposition franchi, nous entendîmes le bruit d'une terrible discussion. Un vieux Monsieur, juste dans le centre de la salle, remettait en caisse ses tableaux en déclarant qu'il remporterait tout si les toiles restaient groupées ainsi. La discussion venait de la place du *Torero mort* qu'à cause de sa forme allongée et étroite on avait accroché à la cimaise, sous une grande toile, dans le panneau d'honneur. Très justement Monsieur E. Rouart, gendre de Berthe Morisot et neveu de Manet, se rebiffait, objectant que ce *profane gisant* n'avait pas été fait pour un devant d'autel, que seul le corps allongé, avait donné au peintre l'idée de ce format et qu'il ne

and the harmonies here bite deeply, forming indelible arabesques.

The poem of Guillaume Apollinaire for *Les Mamelles de Tirésias*, full of latent poetry, never descends into humour that is merely skin deep. I still felt convinced of this only yesterday on rereading the proofs of my score.

Therefore it is essential to *sing Les Mamelles* from beginning to end as if it were by Verdi. It will perhaps not be easy to make this understood by interpreters who generally stick to the outward appearance of things.

January 1946

Bernac, when supervising my plans for the grouping together of songs, made every endeavour (as also in the formulation of our *concert programmes*) to place each song with a following one in a manner calculated to show them both in the most favourable light. It is all a question of "the hanging", as essential in music as in painting.

Concerning this I have often recalled the following story: the day before the opening of an exhibition of Manet[78] at the Orangerie[79] some years ago, I lunched with my dear old friend J.-Emile Blanche, a much better painter than he was reputed to be, a man of immense culture and perfect taste. Having been invited to accompany him for the hanging, I accepted with pleasure. Scarcely had we crossed the threshold before we heard the sound of a terrible argument. An old gentleman in the very centre of the gallery was packing up his pictures, saying that he would remove everything if the canvases remained grouped as they were. The argument arose from the placing of the *Torero mort* which, owing to its long narrow shape, had been hung on the line, under a big canvas, in the panel of honour. Quite rightly, Monsieur E. Rouart, son-in-law of Berthe Morisot[80] and nephew of Manet, bridled, objecting that this *secular recumbent figure* had not been made

devait être surmonté par rien.

C'était la vérité même. Accrochée entre deux toiles de moyenne dimension, sur un pan coupé de la salle, la toile prenait une grandeur et une noblesse surprenantes.

Il en va exactement de même pour le groupement d'un numéro de mélodies et pour l'agencement total d'un programme.

Septembre 46

UN POÈME — LE PONT

J'ai toujours aimé la taille de timbre-poste d'UN POÈME qui suggère avec si peu de mots un grand silence et un grand vide. On doit chanter cette mélodie en *quasi-parlando* et terriblement lentement.

LE PONT est certainement un des poèmes d'Apollinaire les plus délicats à mettre en musique. Ce sont généralement ceux qui m'attirent le plus, c'est pourquoi j'ai toujours préféré, pour mon usage personnel, le recueil *Il y a* aux *Alcools*.

Trouvé, en 44, à Noizay la musique du vers « qui vient de loin qui va si loin », en 45, à Larche (Corrèze) « et passe sous le pont léger de leurs paroles ».

Retravaillé, en mai 46, à l'ensemble et fini tout à coup, en Normandie, en juillet pendant un séjour de travail avec Bernac.

J'espère que malgré ce long polissage, LE PONT donne l'impression d'une coulée aisée.

Il fallait, avant tout, rendre l'impression palpitante de l'eau et de la conversation audessus de l'eau, conversation qui devient « le pont de leurs paroles ».

Le jour, et ce jour-là seulement, où j'ai trouvé la façon de traduire, intelligiblement, la redoutable incidente « c'est pour

for an altar piece, that the length of the body had alone given the painter the idea of this shape and it must not be surmounted by anything.

This was absolutely true. Hung between two canvases of smaller size on a side section of the gallery, the canvas took on a surprising grandeur and nobility.

It is exactly the same with the grouping of a number of songs and the total arrangement of a programme.

September 1946

UN POÈME — LE PONT
[A POEM — THE BRIDGE]

I have always liked the postage-stamp size of 'Un Poème' which expresses in so few words a great silence and a great emptiness. This song must be sung *quasi-parlando* and terribly slowly.

'Le Pont' is certainly one of the most ticklish of Apollinaire's poems to set to music. It is these that generally attract me the most, that is why I have always preferred for my personal use the collection *Il y a* to the *Alcools*.

I found, in 1944, at Noizay the music for the line "qui vient de loin qui va si loin", in 1945, at Larche (Corrèze) "et passe sous le pont léger de leurs paroles".

I worked again at the whole song in May 1946 and finished it in one go in Normandy in July, during a spell of rehearsing with Bernac.

I hope that despite this long polishing, 'Le Pont' gives the impression of an easy flow. It needed, above all, to give the palpitating impression of the water and of the conversation above the water, conversation that becomes "the bridge of their words".

The day, and that day only, when I solved the problem of expressing intelligibly the formidably difficult "c'est pour toi seule que le sang coule", I ventured to write this song.

toi seule que le sang coule », je me suis risqué à écrire cette mélodie.

La dédicace, à la mémoire de Radiguet, est très significative sur le ton « *bords de la Marne* » de cette mélodie.

Jouer LE PONT très égal, d'un seul mouvement, sans *rubato*, et surtout sans ralentir le piano solo de la fin.

Mesdames les accompagnatrices, voulez-vous être assez aimables, je vous prie, pour ne jamais oublier que dans un accompagnement (après tout, pourquoi est-ce qu'on dit accompagnement?) il y a le *chant* du piano et *son accompagnement* propre.

Exemple: (MONTPARNASSE).

Imaginons ce passage transporté à l'orchestre, un cor jouant les notes marquées d'une croix et le reste aux cordes. Cela ne deviendrait-il pas un chant et son accompagnement?

Les compositeurs sont souvent, je m'excuse, les meilleurs accompagnateurs pour les mélodies. Qui ne se souvient d'André Caplet accompagnant les *Ariettes oubliées*, de Reynaldo Hahn, inégalable dans Gounod, Bizet et tous les premiers Fauré? Le secret me semble simple. Nous savons ce qu'il y a dans une musique et nous devinons l'*aura* que nulle notation ne peut rendre.

The dedication, to the memory of Radiguet,[81] is very relevant to the "bords de la Marne" atmosphere of this song.

Play 'Le Pont' very evenly, at a constant *tempo*, without *rubato*, and above all without slowing down the piano solo at the end.

Lady accompanists, will you be so kind, I beg you, never to forget that in an accompaniment (after all, why is it called an accompaniment?) there is the *song* of the piano and its *own accompaniment*.

Example: ('Montparnasse')

Let us imagine this passage given to the orchestra, a horn playing the notes marked with a cross and the rest on the strings. Would that not become a song and its accompaniment?

Composers are often — forgive me — the best accompanists for songs. Who does not remember André Caplet★ accompanying the *Ariettes oubliées*; or Reynaldo Hahn,★ unequalled as accompanist in Gounod,★ Bizet★ and all the early Fauré songs? The secret seems simple to me. We know what there is in the music and we divine the *aura* that no notation can convey.

LE DISPARU

C'est une manière de « lied-chanson » style Môme Piaf. Un rythme immuable, celui de la valse-boston, passe par trois couleurs: le bal musette, la volée de cloches, la marche funèbre. Le poème de Desnos est plus suggestif que réellement de qualité. Nous sommes loin d'Éluard ou Apollinaire.

Si le pianiste ne respecte pas l'indication liminaire: baigné de pédales, les batteries à peine effleurées, les blanches pointées, un peu en dehors, la partie est perdue.

MAIN DOMINÉE PAR LE CŒUR

J'aime spécialement MAIN DOMINÉE PAR LE CŒUR, sur un poème de Paul Éluard.

> *Main dominée par le cœur*
> *Cœur dominé par le lion*
> *Lion dominé par l'oiseau*
>
> *L'oiseau qu'efface un nuage*
> *Le lion que le désert grise*
> *Le cœur que la mort habite*
> *La main refermée en vain*

LE DISPARU
[THE ONE WHO DISAPPEARED]

This is a type of "Lied-chanson" [popular song] in the style of Môme Piaf.★ An immutable rhythm, that of the Boston waltz, passes through three colours: the dance with accordion band, the peal of bells, the funeral march. The poem by Desnos[82] is allusive rather than of true quality. We are far from Éluard and Apollinaire.

If the pianist does not observe the preliminary indication: bathed in pedals, the chords scarcely separated, the minims (half notes) dotted, brought out a little, the game is lost.

☙❧

MAIN DOMINÉE PAR LE CŒUR
[HAND RULED BY THE HEART]

I particularly like 'Main dominée par le cœur', on a poem by Paul Éluard.

> Hand ruled by the heart
> heart ruled by the lion
> lion ruled by the bird

> The bird that a cloud effaces
> the lion intoxicated by the desert
> the heart where death abides
> the hand closed in vain

Aucun secours tout m'échappe
Je vois ce qui disparaît
Je comprends que je n'ai rien
Et je m'imagine à peine

Entre les murs une absence
Puis l'exil dans les ténèbres
Les yeux purs la tête inerte

J'ai noté déjà ce détail capital, à savoir que je ne transpose jamais, pour rendre ma tâche plus aisée, le ton dans lequel j'ai trouvé la musique d'un vers, au hasard du poème. Il s'ensuit que mes modulations passent parfois par le trou d'une souris.

Ici, ayant commencé cette mélodie au premier vers et sachant comment serait la musique du dernier, j'ai dompté les modulations au profit direct des mots. Deux arabesques de sept vers allant d'ut en ut, avec le ton de ré comme point le plus haut (atteint chaque fois par des degrés différents) forment j'estime un tout logique.

Durant les sept premiers vers les mots remontent si joliment à leur source qu'Éluard m'avait proposé le titre (trop mystérieux pour un public): « La Gamme ». J'ai préféré Main dominée par le cœur.

L'interprétation de cette mélodie au rythme fauréen, celui du *Don silencieux*, est sans histoire.

Quelle mélodie divine que « Les Adieux de l'Hôtesse Arabe » de Bizet. Si on ne l'a pas entendue interprétée par Ninon Vallin et Reynaldo Hahn, on ne sait pas ce qu'on a perdu.

No help all escapes me
I see that which disappears
I realise that I have nothing
and I barely imagine myself

An absence between walls
then the exile into the darkness
the eyes pure the head inert

I have already mentioned this essential point, that once the music for a line of a poem has come to me, I never transpose the key in order to make my task easier at the expense of the poem. It follows that my modulations pass at times through a mouse-hole.

Here, having begun this song with the first line and knowing what the music of the last line was to be, I have manipulated the modulations to the direct benefit of the words. Two arabesques of seven lines passing from C to C, with the key of D as the highest (reached each time by different degrees) form in my estimation a logical whole.

During the first seven lines the words return so delightfully to their source, that Éluard proposed a title for me (too enigmatic for the public): 'La Gamme' ['The gamut']. I preferred 'Main dominée par le cœur'.

The interpretation of this song, with its rhythm that recalls Fauré (that of *Don silencieux*), presents no problem.

August 28th, Noizay

What a divine song 'Les Adieux de l'Hôtesse Arabe' by Bizet is. Those who have not heard it interpreted by Ninon Vallin★ and Reynaldo Hahn do not know what they have missed.

87

Comme c'est étrange de penser que les autres mélodies du recueil, à l'exception d'une ou deux, soient si inférieures.

Quel chemin parcouru d'ailleurs entre *La Jolie Fille de Perth* et *Carmen*. Ici, Bizet a su varier, dans le détail, la mélodie à couplets. C'est souvent ce qui manque chez Gounod.

❧

8 septembre 46

Je ne me lasse pas de jouer et rejouer Moussorgski. C'est inouï ce que je lui dois. On ne le sait pas assez.

C'est honnête à moi de l'écrire ici.

Les *Enfantines* et la « Visite d'Anna Karenine à son fils » sont, à mes yeux, l'équivalent pour l'enfance russe des fillettes de Renoir et de Proust pour l'enfance française de la fin du XIXe siècle. J'aurais cité Chardin pour un autre siècle, plus simple, plus naïf, où les jouets étaient un petit volant, de vieilles cartes à jouer, une simple toupie.

❧

PAUL ET VIRGINIE

Ces quelques vers de Radiguet ont toujours eu pour moi une saveur magique.

En 1920 je les avais mis en musique, je ne sais plus comment. Autant qu'il m'en souvienne, j'ai retrouvé la courbe du

How strange it is that the other songs of the collection, with the exception of one or two, should be so inferior. Moreover, what a distance was covered between *La Jolie Fille de Perth* and *Carmen*. Here, Bizet knew how to vary a strophic song in detail. That is often what is missing in Gounod.

⦿⦿

I never tire of playing and replaying Mussorgsky. It is extraordinary how much I owe to him. More than is realized.

To be honest I must write it here.

In my eyes the *Children's Songs* and the 'Visit by Anna Karenina to her Son' are for Russian childhood what the little girls of Renoir and Proust are for French childhood at the end of the nineteenth century. I would cite Chardin[83] for a different century, simpler, more naïve, where the toys are a little shuttlecock, some old playing cards, a simple top.

⦿⦿

PAUL ET VIRGINIE

These few lines of Radiguet have always had a magical savour for me.

In 1920 I set them to music. I don't remember in what manner. As far as I can recall, the curve of the first line came to

premier vers et, à peu près, le déclenchement des quatre suivants, mais à cette époque, faute de contrôle, je m'étais mis à bafouiller, tandis qu'aujourd'hui je crois avoir trouvé le moyen de progresser, sans moduler réellement, jusqu'à cet arrêt brusque, ce silence, qui rend imprévue et comme perchée tout au haut d'un arbre, cette ultime modulation, sans préparation, en ut dièse. J'ai beaucoup repensé à Radiguet ces temps-ci, à propos du PONT, à propos du *Diable au corps* que l'on va tourner et dont j'aurais tant aimé faire la musique. Je pensais qu'elle était échue, comme de juste, à Auric le meilleur ami de Radiguet. Hélas non.

J'ai regardé de près ces jours-ci les autres poèmes des *Joues en feu*. Seul, PAUL ET VIRGINIE m'a paru possible à mettre en musique.

Une journée de pluie, beaucoup de mélancolie m'ont fait trouver ici le ton que je crois juste. Je pense qu'il est utile de bien prendre en considération la mise en page des poésies modernes. C'est ainsi que j'ai eu l'idée de respecter le blanc typographique avant « elle rajeunit ».

Si l'on ne garde pas le *tempo* toujours strictement le même, cette petite mélodie, faite d'un peu de musique de beaucoup de tendresse et d'un silence est fou-tu-e.

TROIS CHANSONS DE LORCA

Comme j'ai de la peine à témoigner musicalement de ma passion pour Lorca! Ma sonate pour piano et violon, dédiée à sa mémoire, est hélas, du très médiocre Poulenc, et ces trois mélodies sont de peu de poids dans mon œuvre vocale.

La dernière mélodie a le défaut d'être « noblement » française tandis qu'elle aurait dû être « gravement » espagnole.

me and very nearly that of the following four, but at that period, lacking technical control, I ran into difficulties, whereas today I believe I have found the means to progress without any real modulation as far as that sudden pause, that silence, which makes the ultimate unprepared modulation into C sharp unexpected and as though perched right on the top of a tree.

Lately I have been giving much thought to Radiguet, apropos of 'Le Pont', apropos of *Le Diable au corps* which is going to be filmed and for which I should have so much liked to write the music. I thought it was assigned, quite rightly, to Auric, Radiguet's best friend. Alas no!

I have been having a closer look of late at the other poems of the *Joues en feu*. 'Paul et Virginie' alone seemed to me possible to set to music.

One rainy day a feeling of great melancholy helped me to find the tone that I believe to be right. I think it is useful to bear carefully in mind how modern poems are placed on the page. It was this that gave me the idea of respecting the blank space in the printing of the poem before "elle rajeunit".

If the *tempo* is not maintained strictly throughout, this small song, made of a little music, of much tenderness and of one silence, is ruined.

∽∾

TROIS CHANSONS DE LORCA
[THREE SONGS BY LORCA][84]

What difficulty I have in proving musically my passion for Lorca! My sonata for piano and violin, dedicated to his memory, is, alas, very mediocre Poulenc, and these three songs are of little importance in my vocal work.

The last song has the defect of being "nobly" French whilst it ought to have been "gravely" Spanish.

∽∾

. . . MAIS MOURIR (Éluard)

J'aime cette mélodie composée à la mémoire de Nush Éluard. Les mains de Nush étaient si belles que ce poème m'a semblé tout spécialement destiné à les évoquer.

HYMNE (Racine)

Il y a dans cet *hymne* des coins qui me satisfont assez, d'autres que j'aurais souhaités plus souples.

Il est impossible de transposer musicalement des alexandrins lorsqu'on n'en sent pas le rythme d'*une façon vivante*. C'est mon cas.

Avril 52

CALLIGRAMMES

J'écris ces lignes quatre ans après avoir composé ce recueil (48) ce qui me permet de le juger froidement. Oserais-je écrire que j'y tiens. Il représente pour moi l'aboutissement de tout un ordre de recherches quant à la transposition musicale d'Apollinaire. Plus je feuillette ses volumes, plus je sens que je n'y trouve plus ma pâture. Non pas que j'aime moins la poésie d'Apollinaire (je ne l'ai jamais tant aimée) mais j'ai l'impression que j'ai épuisé tout ce qui m'y convenait. En 48 je me suis donc attaqué aux CALLIGRAMMES. Comme chez moi l'inspiration (qu'on me pardonne ce mot) survient toujours d'associations d'idées, CALLIGRAMMES se rattachera toujours à ce printemps de 1918 où, avant de monter au front, j'avais acheté

. . . MAIS MOURIR (Éluard)
[. . . BUT TO DIE]

I like this song composed in memory of Nush Éluard.[85] Nush's hands were so beautiful that this poem seems to me quite specially intended to evoke them.

HYMNE (Racine)

There are parts of this *hymn* which satisfy me well enough, others where I would have liked more suppleness. It is impossible to set alexandrines to music when the rhythm is not felt in *a living mode*. This is how I see it.

April 1952

CALLIGRAMMES
[CALLIGRAMS]

I write these lines four years after composing this collection (1948) which allows me to pass a cool judgment. Dare I say that I rate it highly? For me it represents the culmination of a whole range of experiments in setting Apollinaire to music. The more I turn the pages of his volumes, the more I feel that I shall no longer find what I need. Not that I like the poetry of Apollinaire any less (indeed I have never liked it more), but I feel that I have drawn from it all that is suitable for my purposes. In 1948 I began on *Calligrammes*. As with me, inspiration (forgive me for using the word) arises always from an association of ideas, *Calligrammes* will always be connected with that springtime of 1918 when, before leaving for the

chez Adrienne Monnier le volume du *Mercure*.

J'étais alors dans une section de D.C.A. en formation au Tremblay. Une fois de plus le hasard me ramenait aux bords de la Marne de mon enfance. Lorsque nous ne sautions pas « en fausse perm » dans le tramway de Vincennes je finissais mes journées dans des petits bistrots de Nogent.

C'est très exactement dans l'un de ceux-ci que j'ai contact avec le volume d'Apollinaire mêlant ainsi ce que j'allais vivre aux fictions poétiques des CALLIGRAMMES. En souvenir de ce passé, j'ai dédié chacune des mélodies à des amis d'alors et à cette jolie Jacqueline Apollinaire que j'avais aperçue en 1917 à Montparnasse avec Guillaume et Picasso, et pour laquelle j'ai aujourd'hui tant d'affection. Du point de vue technique c'est dans le domaine du raffinement de l'écriture pianistique que j'ai poussé l'aventure essayant dans IL PLEUT d'obtenir une manière de calligramme musical.

La première mélodie: L'ESPIONNE commence sur un rythme que j'ai employé souvent dans des mélodies d'Éluard, mais tout de suite le ton est différent, plus sensuel ici que lyrique. J'estime que « mais la vois-tu — cette mémoire — les yeux bandés — prête à mourir » avec son rythme régulier mais *haché* est une de mes plus *exactes* prosodies.

AUSSI BIEN QUE LES CIGALES me plaît par son ton à mi-chemin entre la chanson (gaillarde ou villageoise) et la mélodie propre. Comme souvent, chez Apollinaire, le poème court vite son chemin pour buter contre une *coda* d'un autre rythme, je crois avoir assez bien traduit « La joie adorable de la paix solaire » par un rythme qui se souvient du soleil des *Animaux modèles*.

Nous arrivons à VOYAGE, *certainement* une des deux ou trois mélodies auxquelles je tiens le plus.

Très *supérieur* à SANGLOTS dont certaines incidentes me pèseront toujours, par le truchement des modulations impré-vues et sensibles, VOYAGE va de l'émotion au silence en passant par la mélancolie et l'amour. Il faut l'accompagner avec beaucoup de pédale, estomper, comme je l'ai sans cesse répété, les batteries et chanter intensément, aussi doucement

front, I bought at Adrienne Monnier's[86] the volume of *Le Mercure*.

At that time I was in an anti-aircraft section, stationed at Tremblay. Once again chance led me to the banks of the Marne of my childhood. When we were not leaping on to the nearest Vincennes tramway taking French leave, I would end each day in the little bistros of Nogent. It was actually in one of these bistros that I first read the volume of Apollinaire, thus blending what I was going to live through with the poetic inventions of *Calligrammes*.

In memory of the past I dedicated each one of the songs to friends of those days and to pretty Jacqueline Apollinaire[87], whom I had first seen in 1917 at Montparnasse with Guillaume and Picasso, and for whom today I feel so much affection. From the technical point of view it is in the field of refinement in piano writing that I was exploring, attempting in 'Il pleut' to achieve a kind of musical calligram.

The first song, 'L'Espionne', begins in a rhythm that I have often used in the Éluard songs, but immediately the colour is different, more sensuous here, than lyrical. I feel that "mais la vois-tu — cette mémoire — les yeux bandés — prête à mourir" with its rhythm regular, but *broken*, is one of my most *exact* prosodies.

I like 'Aussi bien que les cigales' because of its style midway between the "chanson" (ribald or folk) and a true "mélodie". As often with Apollinaire, the poem goes quickly on its way to conclude with a *coda* in another rhythm. I think I have succeeded rather well in expressing "La joie adorable de la paix solaire" in a rhythm that recalls the sunshine of the *Animaux modèles*.

We arrive at 'Voyage', *certainly* one of the two or three songs which I value most.

Greatly superior to 'Sanglots', of which certain points will always trouble me. By the interjection of unexpected and sensitive modulations, 'Voyage' goes from emotion to silence in passing through melancholy and love. It must be accompanied with a great deal of pedal, to soften, as I ceaselessly

au piano qu'à la voix.

« La douce nuit » et la phrase qui suit doivent être *pp*.

« C'est ton visage » doucement et soudainement *f*, comme lorsque des nuages dévoilent tout à coup un rayon lunaire. La fin, c'est pour moi le silence d'une nuit de juillet, lorsque, de la terrasse de ma maison d'enfance de Nogent, j'écoutais, au loin, les trains qui « partaient en vacances » (c'est ainsi que je m'exprimais alors).

❧

MAZURKA
(*Mouvements du cœur* — Vilmorin)

A la manière de Poulenc par un Poulenc qu'une telle aventure rasait.

❧

1950

LA FRAÎCHEUR ET LE FEU

(Éluard)

Indiscutablement mes mélodies les plus concertées. J'ai tant écrit de mélodies jusqu'à ce jour que le goût m'en est passé et que j'en écrirai sans doute de moins en moins. Si celles-ci sont réussies, et je crois qu'elles le sont, c'est qu'un problème technique stimulait mon appétit. Il ne s'agit pas en réalité d'un cycle mais d'*un seul poème* mis en musique, par tronçons séparés, exactement comme le poème est imprimé. Une unité rythmique (deux *tempi*, un rapide, un lent) est à la base de la construction. Le poème progressant admirablement il m'a été facile de prendre, comme point culminant, l'avant-dernière

repeat, the harmonies and to make the piano sing as intensely and as smoothly as the voice.

"La douce nuit" and the phrase which follows must be *pp*.

"C'est ton visage" tenderly and suddenly *forte*, as though the clouds had all at once unveiled a ray of moonlight. The end is for me the silence of a night in July, when, on the terrace of my childhood home at Nogent, I heard in the distance the trains "that were leaving on holiday" (as I used to think then).

◎◎

MAZURKA
(*Mouvements du coeur* — Vilmorin)
[THE HEART'S IMPULSE]

In the style of Poulenc by a Poulenc who was bored by an affair like this.

◎◎

1950

LA FRAÎCHEUR ET LE FEU
[THE COOLNESS AND THE FIRE]
(Éluard)

Indisputably the most integrated of my song cycles. I have written so many songs up to now that I have lost my inclination for them, and doubtless I shall write less and less of them. If these are successful, and I believe they are, it is because a technical problem stimulated my appetite. In reality it is not so much a cycle as *one single poem* set to music in separate sections exactly as the poem is printed. A rhythmic unity (two *tempi*, one rapid, one slow) lies at the base of the construction. The admirable progression of the poem made it easy for me to take as the culminating point the last song but one ('Homme

mélodie (HOMME AU SOURIRE TENDRE). Un certain côté litanies chez Éluard (*Liberté* en est le plus admirable exemple) rejoint chez moi mon sens religieux. Il y a d'ailleurs une pureté mystique chez Éluard. Ces mélodies sont terriblement difficiles à bien exécuter.

Je crains, après Bernac, de ne plus jamais les entendre dans leur *mesure exacte*. Le piano ici est décanté à l'extrême. Pensé une fois de plus à Matisse. C'est à une note près, à une respiration près. C'est pourquoi les temps de pauses, entre les mélodies, ne sont pas laissés au hasard. Les mouvements de métronome sont *implacables*. Il faut remonter ce mécanisme avec une froide précision puis, sûr de soi, tout oublier et avoir l'air d'improviser en n'écoutant plus que l'instinct.

Ces mélodies sont dédiées à Stravinsky parce qu'en quelque sorte elles sont issues de lui. La troisième emprunte en effet le tempo et le sens harmonique de la cadence finale de la *Sérénade en la pour piano*.

Mai 54

Si je n'ai pas écrit de mélodies depuis LA FRAÎCHEUR ET LE FEU c'est que d'autres formes musicales m'ont spécialement accaparé: la musique religieuse et le drame lyrique.

Le style vocal du *Stabat* ou celui du *Dialogue des Carmélites* est en effet aussi loin de la mélodie que le quatuor à cordes l'est de l'orchestre à cordes. Tout à coup, en avril et mai 54, j'ai composé, j'allais dire presque à mon insu, trois mélodies.

A l'époque du BAL MASQUÉ j'avais pensé introduire dans cette cantate le poème de Max Jacob JOUER DU BUGLE mais je dus y renoncer car cela faisait double emploi avec LA DAME AVEUGLE.

Complété par l'extravagant VOUS N'ÉCRIVEZ PLUS si typiquement Max Jacob, je lui ai donné, en 54, le super-titre de PARISIANA qui situe l'atmosphère parigote de l'ensemble.

Il n'y a rien à dire de spécial qui n'ait été déjà dit pour ce

au sourire tendre'). There is something of the litany in Éluard (*Liberté*[88] is the most admirable example of this) which blends with my own religious feeling. There is, besides, a mystical purity in Éluard. These songs are terribly difficult to perform well. I fear that, after Bernac, I shall never hear them attain the golden mean. The piano here is economical to a degree. I thought once again of Matisse. Each note, each breath is important. That is why the timing of the pauses between the songs is not left to chance. The metronomic speeds are *implacable*. The technical performance must be rehearsed again and again with cold precision; then, sure of oneself, forget it all and give the impression of improvising and being led purely by intuition.

These songs are dedicated to Stravinsky because in a kind of way they stem from him. The third one, in fact, borrows the *tempo* and the harmonic progression from the final cadence of his Serenade in A for piano.

May 1954

If I have not written any songs since *La Fraîcheur et le feu* it is because other music has particularly taken up my time: religious music and opera.

The vocal style of the *Stabat*[89] or that of the *Dialogues des Carmélites*[90] is in fact as far removed from the song as the string quartet is from the string orchestra. All of a sudden, in April and May 1954, I composed, I was going to say almost without knowing it, three songs.

At the period of the *Bal masqué* I had been thinking of introducing into the cantata the poem by Max Jacob 'Jouer du bugle' but I had to give up the idea because it would have duplicated 'La Dame aveugle'.

Coupled with the absurd 'Vous n'écrivez plus', so typically Max Jacob, I gave it in 1954 the overall title of *Parisiana*, which placed the whole work, in the ambience of Paris.

genre de fantaisies.

JOUER DU BUGLE est plus musical que VOUS N'ÉCRIVEZ PLUS à cause de sa chute doucement émue.

La troisième mélodie est écrite sur un poème d'Apollinaire extrait d'*Alcools*: ROSEMONDE.

C'est une mélodie sans histoire avec une assez jolie ritournelle finale.

∞⊘

Septembre 56

Tout de même, je l'ai écrit ce cycle: LE TRAVAIL DU PEINTRE dont j'avais parlé à Paul Éluard, quelques mois avant sa mort.

Les sept poèmes qui composent ce recueil sont extraits du volume *Voir*. J'ai pensé que cela pourrait renouveler mes mélodies de *peindre musicalement*: Picasso, Chagall, Braque, Gris, Klee, Miró, Villon.

Lorsque j'avais parlé à Éluard de mon projet je lui avais demandé un poème sur Matisse, que j'adore. Paul me l'avait un peu promis. Je dis un peu car il ne partageait pas ma passion pour ce peintre. Dans mon esprit, Matisse devait clore le cycle dans la joie et le soleil. Aujourd'hui Villon le termine lyriquement et sombrement.

GRIS est la mélodie que j'avais esquissée en premier il y a plusieurs années. J'ai toujours beaucoup admiré ce peintre et beaucoup aimé l'homme, cet honnête et malchanceux Juan qui ne commence qu'aujourd'hui à prendre la place qu'il mérite. Picasso ouvre le recueil: A tout seigneur, tout honneur. Son thème initial, également trouvé voici longtemps, a servi de *souche* pour le thème de la mère Marie dans les *Dialogues des Carmélites*.

Ici, comme dans mon opéra, il prend un ton orgueilleux qui convient bien au modèle.

Cette mélodie, en ut majeur, rappelle, de très loin, le début de TEL JOUR TELLE NUIT, seulement bien des années ont passé et,

There is nothing special to say that I have not already said about this type of fantasy.

'Jouer du bugle' is more musical than 'Vous n'écrivez plus' because of its tenderly affecting ending.

The third song that I wrote at this time is on a poem by Apollinaire taken from *Alcools*: 'Rosemonde'.

It is a song of no great importance with a rather pretty final *ritornello*.

September 1956

Nevertheless I have written this cycle: *Le Travail du peintre*, about which I spoke to Paul Éluard some months before his death.

The seven poems that compose this collection are taken from the volume *Voir*. I thought it would stimulate my work to *paint musically*: Picasso, Chagall, Braque, Gris, Klee, Miró, Villon.[91]

When I spoke to Éluard about my project I asked him for a poem on Matisse, whom I adore. Paul half promised me. I say half promised because he did not share my passion for this painter. To my mind, Matisse should have closed the cycle in joy and sunshine. As it is, Villon ends it lyrically and gravely.

'Gris' is the song that I had first sketched out several years ago. I have always greatly admired this painter and very much liked him as a man, this worthy and unfortunate Juan who is only now beginning to take the place he deserves. Picasso opens the collection: Honour to whom honour is due. Its initial theme, likewise found a long time ago, served as *root-stock* for the theme of Mother Marie in the *Dialogues des Carmélites*.

Here, as in the opera, it takes on a tone of pride well suited to the subject.

This song, in C major, very distantly recalls the beginning of *Tel jour telle nuit*, but many years have passed since then, and

pour le musicien, ut majeur ne veut plus dire bonheur paisible.

C'est le déroulement de la prosodie, avec ses grands enjambements, qui donne à cette mélodie un ton altier. A noter, avant la fin, le blanc vocal devant le mot « renonce » qui, dans mon esprit, souligne le côté impératif de la peinture de Picasso.

CHAGALL est une manière de *scherzo* à la dérive. Des objets hétéroclites passent dans le ciel. Une chute poétique nous ramène à l'être humain.

BRAQUE est la mélodie la plus subtile, la plus fouillée du recueil. Il y a peut-être trop de goût, mais c'est ainsi que je sens Braque.

On devra accompagner avec précision et surtout prendre dès le début, un *tempo* sans lenteur, valable pour la conclusion: « un homme aux yeux légers ».

GRIS. J'ai un faible pour cette mélodie où j'ai pu souligner les équivalences rythmiques qui se trouvent dans le poème:

> *De jour merci, de nuit prends garde*
> *Deux fois le jour, deux fois la nuit*

et encore:

> *Table guitare et verre vide*
> *Table devait se soutenir*

Toute la mélodie est grave et douloureusement mélancolique. La pédale y joue un rôle capital.

KLEE. J'avais besoin ici d'un *presto*. C'est une mélodie sèche qui doit claquer.

MIRÓ. La plus difficile à interpréter avec son passage subit d'un éclat strident à la douceur et au lyrisme, sur les mots « les libellules des raisins ».

Le *céder beaucoup* sur « que je dissipe d'un geste » et la reprise du *tempo* ne s'expliquent pas. Il faut les sentir.

VILLON est avec GRIS ma mélodie préférée. On sait

for the musician, C major no longer means peaceful happiness.

It is the progress of the prosody with its long run-on lines, that gives a lofty tone to this song. Note, before the end, the vocal minim (half note) rest preceding the word "renonce" which to my mind underlines the imperious side of Picasso's painting.

'Chagall' is a kind of rambling *scherzo*. Strange objects pass in the sky. A poetic somersault brings us back to the human being.

'Braque' is the most subtle of the songs, the most detailed of the collection. It is perhaps too mannered, but that is how I feel Braque. It must be accompanied with precision and, above all, from the beginning a *tempo* must be taken that is not too slow, suitable for the conclusion: "un homme aux yeux légers".

'Gris'. I have a liking for this song, in which I have been able to underline the rhythmic similarities that are found in the poem:

> De jour merci, de nuit prends garde
> Deux fois le jour, deux fois la nuit

and again:

> Table guitare et verre vide
> Table devait se soutenir

The whole song is serious and poignantly melancholy. The pedal plays a key role here.

'Klee'. I needed a *presto* here. It is a dry song that must go with a bang.

'Miró'. The most difficult to interpret with its sudden passing from a strident outburst to softness and lyricism on the words, "les libellules des raisins".

The *céder beaucoup* (*molto rallentando*) on "que je dissipe d'un geste" and the return to the *tempo* cannot be explained — it must be felt.

combien j'aime le côté litanies de la poésie d'Éluard. La prosodie de « l'aube, l'horizon, l'eau, l'oiseau, l'homme, l'amour » donne une détente humaine à ce poème si strict et violent.

Tout ce que j'ai déjà dit pour l'interprétation de mes mélodies est valable ici.

C'est plus que jamais un duo où les matières, vocale et pianistique, sont étroitement malaxées.

Il n'est pas question d'un accompagnement.

13 septembre 56

Doda Conrad me demande une mélodie pour les 80 ans de sa mère, Marya Freund.

Sans hésiter je tire de ma bibliothèque le recueil du *Bestiaire* d'Apollinaire car c'est Marya Freund qui a imposé le style *grave* au BESTIAIRE, le seul valable. Puisque, hélas, le temps grignote nos ans, comme la souris, je mets en musique celle d'Apollinaire. Je retrouve tout de suite la mélancolie de mes vingt ans et me crois revenu à Pont-sur-Seine où j'étais troufion en 1919.

Je crois que ma SOURIS est assez gentille.

20 septembre 56

NUAGE

Lorsqu'une amie m'a envoyé, il y a un an, ce poème dactylographié et sans nom d'auteur, je l'avais tout de suite mis de côté dans le cas où . . .

C'est avec un réel plaisir que je viens aujourd'hui de le mettre en musique, car les résonances en sont délicates et

'Villon' is, with 'Gris', the song I like best. It is known how much I like the litanist side of Éluard's poetry. The prosody of "l'aube, l'horizon, l'eau, l'oiseau, l'homme, l'amour" brings human relief to this severe and violent poem.

All that I have already said about the interpretation of my songs is valid here.

It is more than ever a *duo* where the material for voice and piano is closely integrated.

There is no question of "an accompaniment".

September 13th, 1956

Doda Conrad★ asked me for a song for the eightieth birthday of his mother, Marya Freund.★

Without hesitation I took from my shelves the collection of *Le Bestiaire* of Apollinaire, for it is Marya Freund who had imposed the *grave* style on *Le Bestiaire*, the only valid style for it. Since, alas, time nibbles away our years like a mouse, I am setting this poem of Apollinaire to music. Immediately the melancholy I felt when I was twenty comes back to me and I imagine myself back again at Pont-sur-Seine where I was a soldier in 1919.

I think that my 'Souris' is rather pleasing.

September 20th, 1956

NUAGE
[CLOUD]

When a year ago a friend sent me this anonymous, typewritten poem, I put it on one side at once in case . . .

It is with real pleasure that today I have set it to music, for it has delicate and manifold overtones:

The cascade of modulations which underlies:

multiples:

La cascade de modulations qui souligne:

> *Comment retrouver son père*
> *voilé de vent*
> *et comment recueillir*
> *les larmes de sa mère*
> *pour lui donner un nom*

n'est pas sans rappeler la *Valse oubliée* de Liszt, sans doute parce que ces jours-ci j'ai écouté le vieil enregistrement, divin, d'Horowitz.

J'avais pensé, il y a deux ans, ne plus jamais écrire de mélodies, je suis décidément incorrigible.

Le goût de cette forme musicale passe, me dit-on. Tant pis. Vivent Schubert, Schumann, Moussorgski, Chabrier, Debussy, etc . . . etc . . .

20 octobre 56

Qui vous a le mieux chanté? me demandait dernièrement un jeune baryton américain. Je n'hésite pas: Jeanne Bathori pour mes premières mélodies, Marya Freund et Claire Croiza pour LE BESTIAIRE, Suzanne Peignot pour les AIRS CHANTÉS et les CINQ POÈMES de Max Jacob, Suzanne Balguerie pour les FIANÇAILLES POUR RIRE, Madeleine Grey (souvent dans des mélodies paradoxalement peu faites pour elle), Gérard Souzay (PRIEZ POUR PAIX — LE PORTRAIT) et . . . pour tout le reste: Pierre Bernac, bien entendu.

Comment retrouver son père
voilé de vent
et comment recueillir
les larmes de sa mère
pour lui donner un nom

[How to find his father again
veiled with wind
and how to gather
the tears of his mother
to give him a name]

is not without an echo of the *Valse oubliée* of Liszt, no doubt because during these last few days I have been listening to the old recording, divine, of Horowitz.★

Two years ago I had thought that I would never write any more songs; I am certainly incorrigible.

The taste for this musical form is coming to an end, so I am told. So much the worse. Long live Schubert, Schumann, Mussorgsky, Chabrier,★ Debussy,[92] etc . . . etc . . .

October 20th, 1956

Who sings your songs best? I was asked recently by a young American baritone. I do not hesitate: Jane Bathori★ for my first songs, Marya Freund★ and Claire Croiza★ for *Le Bestiaire*, Suzanne Peignot★ for the *Airs chantés* and the *Cinq Poèmes de Max Jacob*, Suzanne Balguerie★ for the *Fiançailles pour rire*, Madeleine Grey★ (often in songs which are, paradoxically, little suited to her), Gérard Souzay★ ('Priez pour paix' and 'Le portrait') and . . . for all the rest: Pierre Bernac,★ of course.

28 novembre 56. Berlin

Je me demandais, ce matin, comment expliquer à un critique allemand le côté banlieusard de ma musique, quand me promenant avec lui, dans les rues de Berlin, j'avisai tout à coup, dans la vitrine d'un libraire, une grande reproduction d'un célèbre tableau de Dufy « Canotiers aux bords de la Marne ».

« Voyez, dis-je: c'est ma musique nogentaise ».

J'ai d'ailleurs toujours pensé que Dufy et moi avions plus d'un point commun.

Mai 59

Pour la dèrnière fois j'ai paru en scène, hier soir, avec Bernac.

Il a chanté mieux que jamais, à ce concert donné chez Gaveau, à l'occasion de mes 60 ans . . .

Le public a fait un *triomphe* à cet artiste exemplaire. Mes doigts tremblaient un peu en attaquant le TRAVAIL DU PEINTRE. Ensuite je me suis ressaisi.

C'est mélancolique la fin d'une si fraternelle association . . .

Août 60

LA COURTE PAILLE

Sur de charmants poèmes de Maurice Carême, à mi-chemin entre Francis Jammes et Max Jacob, j'ai composé sept courtes mélodies pour Denise Duval ou, plus exactement, pour que Denise Duval les chante à son petit garçon âgé de six ans. Ces croquis tour à tour mélancoliques ou malicieux sont sans prétention. Il faut les chanter avec tendresse. C'est la plus sûre façon de toucher le cœur des enfants.

November 28th, 1956. Berlin.

While walking with a German music critic in the streets of Berlin this morning, I was wondering how to explain to him the evocation in my music of Parisian suburbia, when suddenly I caught sight in a bookshop window of a big reproduction of a celebrated picture by Dufy:[91] 'Boatmen on the banks of the Marne'.

"Look," I said, "that is my Nogent music."

I have always thought, moreover, that Dufy and I had more than a little in common.

❧

May 1959

Yesterday evening I appeared on the platform for the last time with Bernac.

He sang better than ever at the concert at Salle Gaveau to celebrate my sixtieth birthday . . .

The public accorded a *triumph* to this exemplary artist. My fingers trembled a little in beginning *Le Travail du peintre*. Then I gained control of myself.

The end of such a fraternal association is very sad . . .

❧

August 1960

LA COURTE PAILLE
[THE SHORT STRAW]

On some charming poems by Maurice Carême,[93] half-way between Francis Jammes[94] and Max Jacob, I have composed seven short songs for Denise Duval or, more exactly, for Denise Duval to sing to her little boy of six. These sketches, by turns sad or mischievous, are unpretentious. They should be sung tenderly. That is the surest way to touch the heart of a child.

❧

Septembre 60, Noizay

J'ai beaucoup rejoué tous ces jours-ci d'anciennes mélodies. Je ne comprends pas qu'on chante si rarement mes CINQ POÈMES DE MAX JACOB. C'est à coup sûr un de mes recueils les plus authentiques. J'y tiens certainement davantage qu'aux FIANÇAILLES POUR RIRE, plus fabriqué.

Peut-être ai-je été dans ce Journal exagérément sévère pour l'AIR CHAMPÊTRE et l'AIR VIF. Sûrement pas assez pour les POÈMES DE RONSARD.

☙❧

Octobre 60

Tous mes mouvements métronomiques, réglés avec Bernac, sont exacts.

☙❧

3 avril 1961

LA DAME DE MONTE-CARLO

Tout à coup un fantôme envahit ma musique. Monte-Carlo. Monte-Carlo, la Venise de mes vingt ans! . . . Acheté, par hasard, à Cannes, le *Théâtre de poche* de Jean Cocteau, il y a une quinzaine de jours. Je ne connaissais pas *La dame de Monte-Carlo* écrit pour Marianne Oswald, il y a plus de vingt ans. Ce monologue m'enchante car il ressuscite pour moi les années 1923–1925 où je vivais, avec Auric, à Monte-Carlo, dans l'ombre impériale de Diaghilev. *Les Fâcheux* et *Les Biches* ont été créés en janvier 1924. Les ai-je assez approchées ces vieilles épaves, faucheuses de mises. Je dois avouer, pour être honnête, qu'avec Auric, je les ai même croisées, au Mont-de-Piété où notre imprudente jeunesse nous conduisit une ou deux fois. Comme c'est curieux que ma collaboration avec Jean Cocteau soit à retardement. De même que pour *La*

September 1960, Noizay

I have spent much time during these last days playing my old songs again. I fail to understand why my *Cinq Poèmes de Max Jacob* are so seldom sung. There is no doubt at all that it is one of my most genuine collections. I certainly much prefer it to *Fiançailles pour rire*, which is more contrived.

Perhaps in this diary I have been over severe about the 'Air champêtre' and the 'Air vif'. Certainly not severe enough for the *Poèmes de Ronsard*.

〰️

October 1960

All my metronomic speeds, worked out with Bernac, are exact.

〰️

April 3rd, 1961

LA DAME DE MONTE–CARLO

Suddenly a phantom invaded my music. Monte Carlo. Monte Carlo, the Venice of my twenties! . . . Bought by chance at Cannes the *Théâtre de Poche* of Jean Cocteau,★ about a fortnight ago. I did not know *La Dame de Monte-Carlo*,[95] written for Marianne Oswald★ more than twenty years ago. This monologue delighted me because it brought back to me the years 1923–1925 when I lived, together with Auric, in Monte Carlo, in the imperial shadow of Diaghilev.[96] *Les Fâcheux*[97] and *Les Biches* were created in January 1924. I have often enough seen at close quarters those old wrecks of women, light-fingered ladies of the gaming tables. In all honesty I must admit that Auric and I even came across them at the pawnshop where our imprudent youth led us once or twice.

How strange it is that my collaboration with Jean Cocteau

Voix humaine je n'aurais pas songé, en son temps, à mettre en musique ce texte. Je pense qu'accouplée avec l'air des *Mamelles de Tirésias*, LA DAME DE MONTE-CARLO peut constituer un excellent numéro pour Denise Duval à laquelle je l'ai dédiée.

Conçu pour voix de soprano et orchestre par deux, ce *monologue* présentait une difficulté majeure: échapper à la monotonie tout en conservant un rythme immuable. C'est pourquoi j'ai essayé de donner une couleur différente à chaque strophe du poème. Mélancolie, orgueil, lyrisme, violence et sarcasme. Enfin tendresse misérable, angoisse et floc dans la mer.

L'orchestration, assez semblable à celle de *La Voix humaine*, comporte quelques touches furtives de batterie: un vibraphone, employé artificiellement comme au music-hall, une pincée de castagnettes, un coup de tam-tam à la fin.

Il faut chanter LA DAME DE MONTE-CARLO comme la prière de la Tosca! Mais oui!

Je feuillette ce journal avec quelque mélancolie. Le temps n'est plus aux mélodies (du moins pour moi).

J'ai tiré tout ce que *je pouvais* d'Éluard — Apollinaire, Max Jacob, etc . . .

Notre association avec Bernac est terminée. Il me faut chercher ailleurs.

Je note cependant ici deux mélodies oubliées, pour une honnête comptabilité:

DERNIER POÈME de Desnos et UNE CHANSON DE PORCELAINE d'Éluard.

DERNIER POÈME est, je crois, assez réussi. Un critique suisse a écrit que c'était ce que j'avais fait de mieux (sic). Pauvre de moi, pauvre de lui.

UNE CHANSON, composée pour les quatre-vingts ans de Bathori est sans surprise. La seconde partie, proche du TRAVAIL, est bien dessinée.

Et voilà!!!

should come so late. Likewise with *La Voix humaine*.[98] I would not have dreamed, in his time, of putting this text to music. I think that coupled with the solo from *Les Mamelles de Tirésias*, *La Dame de Monte-Carlo* would make an excellent number for Denise Duval, to whom I have dedicated it.

Conceived for a soprano voice and orchestra, this *monologue* presented a major difficulty: how to escape monotony while conserving an immutable rhythm. That is why I have tried to give a different colour to each verse of the poem. Sadness, pride, lyricism, violence and sarcasm. In the end miserable tenderness, anguish and splash into the sea.

The orchestration, rather similar to that of *La Voix humaine*, includes a few stealthy touches of percussion: a vibraphone, used artificially as in a music-hall, a clap of castanets, a beat of a tam-tam at the end.

La Dame de Monte-Carlo should be sung like the prayer of Tosca! Yes, certainly!

I turn the pages of this diary with a certain sadness. The time for songs is no more (at least for me).

I have taken all that *I could* from Éluard, Apollinaire, Max Jacob, etc . . .

The association with Bernac is at an end. I must look to other things.

Nevertheless I am noting here two forgotten songs, to square the account:

'Dernier Poème' by Desnos and 'Une Chanson de porcelaine' by Éluard.

'Dernier Poème' is, I believe, successful enough. A Swiss critic wrote that it is the best thing I have done (sic). Poor me, poor him.

'Une Chanson', composed for the eightieth birthday of Bathori, is nothing out of the way. The second part, a little like 'Travail', is well designed.

And so, that's that!!!

NOTES

These notes are provided for the benefit of English and American readers who may be unfamiliar with the musical and artistic scene in France during the period covered by Poulenc's *Journal*.

More detailed information about, for example, some of the poets whom he mentions, may be found in *Francis Poulenc, the man and his songs*, by Pierre Bernac (Gollancz 1977).

For entries marked ★ see Discographical Appendix.

1. 'Green' is from Debussy's song cycle *Ariettes oubliées*.

2. Gabriel Fauré's Sonata in A major for violin and piano, Op. 13.

3. Valentine Hugo (née Gross) (1887–1968) French painter of partly Polish extraction; married to Jean Hugo, a great-grandson of Victor Hugo. She was one of the group "Les Nouveaux Jeunes", out of which grew "Les Six" (qv★), designing some of the sets for their performances at the Vieux-Colombier. She was a member of the Cocteau –Picasso–Misia Sert circle.
   See under Pierre BERTIN.★

4. Marie Laurencin (1885–1956) French painter; for some time she lived with Guillaume Apollinaire (qv★). At first linked with the Cubist movement she later developed a style of delicately coloured, elegant feminine compositions of great originality. She designed the costumes for Poulenc's ballet *Les Biches*, which was commissioned by Diaghilev and presented by the Russian Ballet at Monte Carlo in 1924. The poems of the songs 'Le Présent' and 'Hier' from *Trois Poèmes de Louise Lalanne* are by Marie Laurencin.

5. Franz Schubert (1797–1828) Austrian composer whose

cycle *Die Winterreise* Poulenc said was a "revelation of his own destiny to be a song writer".

6. Debussy's *Ariettes oubliées* date from 1885-8 and the *Poèmes de Baudelaire* from 1887–90.

7. Fontainebleau is a town thirty-five miles south of Paris surrounded by a forest of the same name. It is the site of a palace, originally built about 1528 by Francis I; in its grounds is a famous "Étang des carpes" (carp-pool), and it is to this that Poulenc refers.

8. Roger de la Fresnaye (1865–1925) French painter; called "the most French of the Cubists". He later joined the "Section d'or", a group which experimented with rhythmic forms and brilliant colours. During the first world war he painted pictures of war scenes.

9. The Médrano was a circus in Montmartre, famous for its Fratellini clowns, often visited by Poulenc and the other members of "Les Six".

10. La Bande à Bonnot (the Bonnot gang), anarchists named after their leader, Jules Joseph Bonnot (1876–1912), who took part in attacks on banks, which they termed "expropriation". Bonnot himself was shot as he was about to be arrested; the other members of the group were arrested in 1913, four being condemned to death and eleven to forced labour.

11. Poulenc often refers to two places in which he had lived: Nogent and Noizay. Nogent-sur-Marne is a village on the outskirts of Paris. His grandparents had a house there and in his early years Poulenc often stayed with them. Noizay is a village in the Touraine; there Poulenc bought a large house in its own grounds as a refuge in which to work away from the distractions of Paris.

12. *Les Biches* is a ballet which Diaghilev commissioned and which received its première in Monte Carlo in 1924.

13. *Mavra* is a one-act opera by Stravinsky. *Les Noces* (see p. 53) is a ballet by him for four singers, four pianos and percussion. See under STRAVINSKY.*

14. Jean Racine (1639–99) French poet and dramatist in whose tragedies humanity is shown as being destroyed by the vanity, ambition, jealousy and passion which it harbours.

15. Maurice Ravel (1875–1937) French composer who wrote two operas — *L'Heure espagnole* and *L'Enfant et les sortilèges*, chamber, piano and orchestral works, and songs and other vocal works. The *Greek songs* which Poulenc mentions (see p. 31) are the *Cinq Mélodies populaires grecques*, traditional songs for which Ravel wrote piano accompaniments in connection with a lecture given by M. D. Calvocoressi in 1904. "The ghost of an Athenian Chopin" is a reference to the *Chants polonais* — traditional Polish melodies with piano accompaniments by Chopin.

16. Jean Moréas (1856–1910) (né Jannis Papadiamantopoulos), a Greek poet who wrote in French, was at first associated with the Symbolists but later founded a neoclassical school known as the "École romane".

17. François de Malherbe (1555–1628) was the Royal Court poet of his time.

18. 'Le Présent' opens with four bars in 3/8 with a comma at the end of each bar indicating a slight break. The rest of the song is in 2/4. The Chopin sonata to which Poulenc refers is the second sonata in B flat minor, Op. 35.

19. Édouard Vuillard (1868–1940) French painter who belonged to the Intimist school, painting mainly interiors and portraits.

20. Pierre Bonnard (1867–1947) French painter who shared a studio with Vuillard and was a fellow Intimist. Misia Sert (Marie Sophie Olga Zenaïde Godebska) (1872–1950) belonged to a noble Polish family which had lost its fortune. A woman of rare beauty, charm and personality,

she was in turn the wife of Thadée Natanson, Alfred Edwards (a millionaire of Turkish extraction who was a prominent figure in artistic and social circles in Paris) and Jose-Maria Sert (a Catalan painter who specialized in murals on a grand scale).

Misia Sert was a great patron of the arts. Ravel dedicated *La Valse* to her.

21. Sidonie Gabrielle Colette (1873–1954) French novelist of childhood, adolescence and the animal world. The libretto of Ravel's opera *L'Enfant et les sortilèges* and the text of Poulenc's song 'Le Portrait' are by Colette.

22. Max Jacob (1876–1944) French avant-garde poet whose works combine mysticism with humour and parody; he was closely associated with Picasso, Apollinaire and their circle. Jewish by birth, he became a Catholic convert. He died in a concentration camp.

23. Modest Petrovich Mussorgky (1839–1881) Russian composer whose best-known works are the opera *Boris Godunov*, *Pictures at an Exhibition* for piano (of which Ravel wrote a famous arrangement for orchestra) and a large number of highly original songs.

24. By "well 'bowed'" Poulenc means a long span of *legato* phrasing.

25. Paul Éluard (pseud. of Eugène Grindel) (1895–1952) French "poet of love", originally a Surrealist and later a communist.

26. Henri Matisse (1869–1954) French painter much influenced by Cézanne and regarded as the principal Fauve artist early in the century.

27. Stéphane Mallarmé (1842–98) French idealist poet who aimed to express not the thing itself but the essence behind it.

28. The critic to whom Poulenc refers was probably R. Aloys Mooser.

29. Édouard Bourdet (1887–1945) French playwright who satirizes social and psychological situations. He invited Poulenc to write incidental music for his play about the loves of Marguerite de Valois, *La Reine Margot*. In addition to pieces for nine wind instruments, drums and keyboard based on dances by Claude Gervaise, which Poulenc entitled *Suite française*, he wrote a song to a text by Ronsard, 'A sa guitare', to be sung by Yvonne Printemps (qv★), who was taking the part of Marguerite. On the stage she sang it accompanied by a harp.

30. The Château de Plessis-les-Tours was built by Louis XI, who died there in 1483.

31. The Bastille, Ménilmontant, Montmartre (see p. 75) and Montparnasse are districts of Paris.

32. La Grande Chartreuse is a monastery founded in 1084 in a valley in the Alps.

33. Philippe de Champaigne (1602–74) Belgian painter, principally of portraits; he lived and died in France.

34. Marie-Blanche de Polignac (Comtesse Jean de Polignac), who was the niece of Princesse Edmond de Polignac (née Singer, a generous patron of the arts), was a close friend of Poulenc's. She sang and recorded as a member of Nadia Boulanger's ensemble. Poulenc dedicated a number of works to her including *Un Soir de neige*, *3 Poèmes de Louise de Vilmorin*, and 'A toutes brides' from *Tel jour telle nuit*; also, to her memory, the *Élégie* for two pianos.

35. "J'aime tes yeux . . ." is from Fauré's 'Chanson d'amour'.

36. Charles-Pierre Baudelaire (1821–67) French poet and critic. In essence a forward-looking poet, he had an immense influence on contemporary poets and those of later generations.

37. Molière (pseud. of Jean-Baptiste Poquelin) (1622–73) French dramatist; his plays ridicule human failings — vanity, pretence, stupidity and pomposity.

38. Thérèse Dorny. French actress; début 1902. Poulenc dedicated his ninth *Improvisation pour piano* to her.

39. Anost, Nevers, Saulieu (see p. 47), Autun and Arnay-le-Duc are towns and villages in the Morvan, in central France.

40. Poulenc's Mass in G major, dedicated to the memory of his father, was first performed in February 1938. See under Ernest BOURMAUCK★.

41. The song 'Je nommerai ton front' is not included in the cycle *Tel jour telle nuit*, though that may have been Poulenc's original intention. In discussing the cycle in his Diary (see p. 35) he inadvertently refers to this song instead of to 'Le Front comme un drapeau perdu'. 'Je nommerai ton front' was published separately, as the second song in *Miroirs brûlants*, and was first performed, by Bernac and Poulenc, in December 1938, nearly two years after *Tel jour telle nuit*.

42. For the *Litanies à la Vierge Noire* and *Motets pour un temps de pénitence* (see p. 59) see under Yvonne GOUVERNÉ.★

43. Charles d'Orléans (1394–1465) French poet; nephew of Charles VI and father of Louis XII. Captured at Agincourt and kept prisoner in England for 25 years. Poet of courtly love.

44. The restaurant at La Grenouillère was the subject of a famous painting by Renoir.

45. Raymonde Linossier (1897–1930) French Dadaist poet, lawyer and orientalist; childhood friend of Poulenc, to whose memory he dedicated *Les Animaux modèles*; to Poulenc she dedicated her *Bibi-la-Bibiste*.

46. The rue de Clichy and the rue d'Athènes are in Montmartre near the Trinité; the Casino de Paris is a music hall in the rue de Clichy.

47. Kamchatka is a peninsula in Siberia; presumably Poulenc means to signify some outlandish place.

48. Christian Bérard (1902–49) French painter and designer; a close friend of Poulenc famous for his stage designs. Poulenc dedicated the *Stabat Mater* to his memory.

49. The Viscomte and Viscomtesse de Noailles were patrons of music who commissioned several of Poulenc's works. He dedicated his *Aubade* for piano and orchestra to them.

50. Friedrich Nietzsche (1844–1900) German philosopher who died insane.

51. Henri Désiré Landru (1869–1922) French murderer, sometimes called "the modern Bluebeard". Alleged to have murdered ten women and a boy and to have disposed of the remains in a stove, he was found guilty on circumstantial evidence and guillotined.

52. Scarpia is the villainous chief of police in Puccini's opera *Tosca*; the part requires a baritone of great power.

53. The Foire du Trône is a Paris fun fair.

54. In France a "serious" song (*Lied* or art-song) is called a "mélodie" and a popular song a "chanson".

55. Arthur Honegger (1892–1955) Swiss composer born in France; a member of "Les Six" (qv★). His musical sympathies were as much German as French; although linked by close ties of friendship to Poulenc, Milhaud and Auric, he moved away from the musical ideals of his youth towards what he described as "music in its most serious and austere aspects". His best known work is the dramatic psalm *Le Roi David*, dating from 1921.

56. Blaise Cendrars (pseud. of Frédéric Sauser) (1887–1961) Franco–Swiss author, many of whose novels and other works are based on his frequent wanderings throughout the world. He was involved in the concerts of the "Nouveaux Jeunes" and "Les Six" (qv*) from about 1916 onwards.

57. Moise Kisling (1891–1953) Polish painter who spent many years in France.

58. André Derain (1880–1954) French painter; a Fauve, much influenced by Cézanne and Matisse.

59. Guy Pierre Fauconnet (1882–1920) French painter; one of the group of "Les Nouveaux Jeunes".

60. The Théâtre du Vieux-Colombier was founded in 1913 in the rue Vieux-Colombier in Paris by Jacques Copeau. During Copeau's absence in America during the first world war it was directed by Jane Bathori (qv*) and there the first public performance of a work by Poulenc — his *Rapsodie nègre* — was given in 1917.

61. The Bobino, a music hall at 20 rue de la Gaîté in the Montparnasse region of Paris, was established in 1880.

62. The Théâtre de l'Empire, originally the Étoile-Palace, was a Paris music hall at 39 avenue de Wagram.

63. Jacques-Emile Blanche (1861–1942) French painter, mainly of portraits.

64. Paul Valéry (1871–1945) French poet and critic. Poulenc set a text by Valéry in the duet for soprano and baritone, with piano accompaniment, entitled *Colloque*, which dates from 1940, but which was not published until 1978.

65. Maurice Maeterlinck (1862–1949) Belgian Symbolist poet and dramatist; works by Debussy and Schönberg were based on his *Pelléas et Mélisande* and by Dukas on his *Ariane et Barbe-Bleue*.

66. From 'Chanson d'Orkenise', the first song in the cycle *Banalités*; Poulenc re-uses the opening phrases in *L'Histoire de Babar, le petit éléphant.*

67. "F.G." is probably Fred Goldbeck, a well-known Paris music critic.

68. *Animaux modèles* is a one-act ballet based on La Fontaine fables, dedicated to the memory of Raymonde Linossier. It was first performed with choreography by Lifar, at the Paris Opéra in 1942.

69. Maurice Fombeure (1906-81) French poet and prose writer whose poetry is akin to folk song.

70. Poulenc's picturesque phrase "bridging song" suggests a trampoline song from which a more serious song can bounce its way into its proper place in the programme.

71. Louis Aragon (1897–1982) French poet, novelist and prose writer; originally a Surrealist he became a communist after visiting the USSR in 1930.

72. Eugène Devéria (1805–65) and his brother Jacques Jean-Marie (1800–57) French traditional painters. Eugène Delacroix (1798–1863) French painter, anti-classicist and a leader of the romantic movement. Alfred de Musset (1810–57) French playwright, poet and novelist, neo-classicist.

73. *Les Mamelles de Tirésias* is an opera by Poulenc with text by Apollinaire based on his play of 1916. It was first produced at the Opéra-Comique in 1947, conducted by Albert Wolff and with Denise Duval (qv★) in the title role.

74. Pablo Picasso (pseud. of Pablo Ruiz Blasco) (1881–1973) Spanish painter.

75. Braque, Georges (1882–1963) French painter.

76. Amedeo Modigliani (1884–1920) Italian painter influenced by Cézanne and Picasso.

77. The Comtesse de Noailles (Anna Elisabeth de Noailles) (née Anna de Bibesco-Brancovan) (1876–1933) was a Rumanian princess who married Comte Mathieu de Noailles. She had a literary salon and belonged to the poetic group known as *La Nouvelle Pléiade*. Some of her poems were among the finest in French literature written by a woman. She was the first woman to be made a *Commandeur de la Légion d'honneur*.

78. Édouard Manet (1832–83) French painter.

79. The Orangerie (Orangery) is a picture gallery in Paris in the Jardins des Tuileries facing the Place de la Concorde.

80. Berthe Morisot (1841–95) French Impressionist painter.

81. Raymond Radiguet (1903–23) French poet and novelist who began his first novel at the age of fourteen. He was greatly influenced and helped by Cocteau, with whom he lived. He was a childhood friend of Poulenc, and they used to go for walks along the banks of the Marne — hence Poulenc's comment on the atmosphere of his song 'Le Pont' and its dedication.
    The music for the film *Le Diable au corps* (see p. 91) was composed by René Cloerec.

82. Robert Desnos (1900–45) French surrealist poet; an exponent of "automatic writing".

83. Jean Baptiste Siméon Chardin (1699–1779) French painter of still-life and domestic interiors.

84. Federico Garcia Lorca (1898–1936) Spanish poet and dramatist.

85. Nusch Éluard, whose name Poulenc sometimes spelt "Nush" or "Nouche", was the wife of Paul Éluard from 1934 until her death in 1946. Poulenc dedicated 'Le Front comme un drapeau perdu' from *Tel jour telle nuit* and 'Mais mourir' to her.

86. Adrienne Monnier (1892–1955) French author. In 1915 she opened a bookshop, "La Maison des Amis des Livres" in Paris, at 7 rue de l'Odéon. She was a close friend of Sylvia Beach, publisher of James Joyce's *Ulysses*, who, with her encouragement, opened an English language bookshop at 12 rue de l'Odéon.

Mlle Monnier held readings of their own works by Jules Romains, Valéry, Apollinaire, Gide, Léon-Paul Fargue, Valéry Larbaud and many others. She also arranged a performance of Satie's *Socrate*, introduced by Cocteau, in which all the parts were sung by Suzanne Balguerie, with Satie himself at the piano.

Poulenc was introduced to Mlle Monnier and her shop by their mutual friend Raymonde Linossier.

87. Jacqueline Apollinaire (née Kolb) was the wife of Guillaume Apollinaire; they were married on 2 May 1918, six months before his death. She died in 1967. She was known as Ruby, or "la jolie rousse", because of her red hair, and is the subject of the last poem in *Calligrammes*, published in April 1918.

88. Éluard's poem 'Liberté' was set to music by Poulenc in his choral work *Figure humaine*.

89. The *Stabat Mater*, dedicated to the memory of Christian Bérard, was first performed at Strasbourg, by Geneviève Moizan (qv★) (soprano) with chorus and orchestra under Fritz Münch, in 1951.

90. *Dialogues des Carmélites* is a three-act opera with a libretto based on a play by Georges Bernanos. It was dedicated to the memory of the composer's mother. The first performance, in Italian, took place at the Scala, Milan on 26 January 1957; the first performance of the original French version was given at the Paris Opéra on 21 June 1957 with a cast which included Denise Duval (qv★), and Pierre Dervaux as conductor.

91. Poulenc had always been attracted to the visual arts, and

his love of painting in particular led him to set Éluard's cycle *Le Travail du peintre* to music. He was especially drawn to the paintings of Matisse and Dufy, and felt that in their different media he and Dufy had much in common. He therefore hoped that Éluard could be persuaded to add to his cycle poems about these two artists; but in this hope he was disappointed and the cycle is based on the following: Georges Braque (1882–1963) French Cubist painter and sculptor; Marc Chagall (1887-1985) Russian painter who lived in France for many years; Juán Gris (1887–1927) Spanish Cubist painter; Paul Klee (1879–1940) Swiss Surrealist painter; Pablo Picasso (1881–1973) Spanish artist who was a dominant influence on the art of the first half of the century; Joan Miró (1893-1983) Spanish Surrealist and abstract painter of great influence; and Jacques Villon (1875–1963) (pseud. of Gaston Duchamp-Villon) French Cubist artist, brother of the Dada artist Marcel Duchamp and the sculptor Raymond Duchamp-Villon.

92. Achille-Claude Debussy (1862–1918) French composer. Poulenc often expressed his love for Debussy's music and the debt he owed to him. In the *Entretiens avec Claude Rostand* he says, "it was Debussy, without question, who awakened me to music", and, "Debussy has always been the composer that I prefer after Mozart; and in the dedication of *Dialogues des Carmélites* he writes, "to the memory of my mother, who revealed to me the music of Debussy, which gave me the desire to write music myself."

93. Maurice Carême (1899-1977) Belgian poet.

94. Francis Jammes (1868–1938) French poet and novelist of the countryside.

95. In *La Dame de Monte-Carlo* an ageing woman, poor and alone, comes for the last time to Monte Carlo. Disillusioned in her hope of winning at the gaming tables, or

even of succeeding in stealing one of the stakes, she ends her miserable life with a leap into the sea. See under Denise DUVAL★.

96. Serge Pavlovich de Diaghilev (1872–1929) Russian impresario who organized concerts of Russian music in Paris from 1907 and operas and ballets from 1908. Among painters who worked for him were Derain, Braque, Picasso, and Marie Laurencin, and among composers Debussy, Ravel, Satie, Richard Strauss, Falla, Prokofiev, Auric, Milhaud, Sauguet and Poulenc (*Les Biches*). His influence on the whole development of the arts in Western Europe was immense.

97. *Les Fâcheux* is a ballet by Georges Auric dating from 1923.

98. *La Voix humaine* is a one-act lyric tragedy, based on Cocteau's monodrama of 1930; it was composed in 1958 and its première took place at the Opéra-Comique in 1959, with Cocteau as designer and producer, Denise Duval (qv★) (soprano) and Georges Prêtre★ (conductor).

LIST OF SONGS BY
FRANCIS POULENC

1918–1919

Le Bestiaire or *Cortège d'Orphée*   (G. Apollinaire)
MAX ESCHIG
1. Le dromadaire
2. La chèvre du Thibet
3. La sauterelle
4. Le dauphin
5. L'écrevisse
6. La carpe

1919

Cocardes   (Jean Cocteau)   MAX ESCHIG
1. Miel de Narbonne
2. Bonne d'enfant
3. Enfant de troupe

1924–1925

Poèmes de Ronsard   HEUGEL
1. Attributs
2. Le tombeau
3. Ballet
4. Je n'ai plus que les os
5. A son page

1926

Chansons gaillardes   (Textes anonymes du XVIIᵉ siècle)
HEUGEL
1. La maîtresse volage
2. Chanson à boire
3. Madrigal
4. Invocation aux Parques

5. Couplets bachiques
6. L'offrande
7. La belle jeunesse
8. Sérénade

1927

Vocalise LEDUC

1927–1928

Airs chantés (J. Moréas) SALABERT
1. Air romantique
2. Air champêtre
3. Air grave
4. Air vif

1930

Épitaphe (Malherbe) SALABERT

1931

Trois poèmes de Louise Lalanne SALABERT
1. Le Présent
2. Chanson
3. Hier

Quatre poèmes (G. Apollinaire) SALABERT
1. L'anguille
2. Carte postale
3. Avant le cinéma
4. 1904

Cinq poèmes (Max Jacob) SALABERT
1. Chanson bretonne
2. Le cimetière
3. La petite servante
4. Berceuse
5. Souric et Mouric

1934

Huit chansons polonaises   SALABERT
1. La couronne
2. Le départ
3. Les gars polonais
4. Le dernier mazour
5. L'adieu
6. Le drapeau blanc
7. La Vistule
8. Le lac

1935

Cinq poèmes   (P. Éluard)   DURAND
1. Peut-il se reposer?
2. Il la prend dans ses bras
3. Plume d'eau claire
4. Rôdeuse au front de verre
5. Amoureuses

A sa guitare   (Ronsard)   DURAND

1937

Tel jour telle nuit   (P. Éluard)   DURAND
1. Bonne journée
2. Une ruine coquille vide
3. Le front comme un drapeau perdu
4. Une roulotte couverte en tuiles
5. A toutes brides
6. Une herbe pauvre
7. Je n'ai envie que de t'aimer
8. Figure de force brûlante et farouche
9. Nous avons fait la nuit

Trois poèmes   (Louise de Vilmorin)   DURAND
1. Le garçon de Liège
2. Au-delà
3. Aux officiers de la Garde Blanche

1938

Deux poèmes   (G. Apollinaire)   SALABERT
   1. Dans le jardin d'Anna
   2. Allons plus vite

Miroirs brûlants   (P. Éluard)   SALABERT
   1. Tu vois le feu du soir
   2. Je nommerai ton front

Le portrait   (Colette)   SALABERT

La grenouillère   (G. Apollinaire)   SALABERT

Priez pour paix   (Charles d'Orléans)   SALABERT

Ce doux petit visage   (P. Éluard)   SALABERT

1939

Bleuet   (G. Apollinaire)   DURAND

Fiançailles pour rire   (Louise de Vilmorin)
SALABERT
   1. La dame d'André
   2. Dans l'herbe
   3. Il vole
   4. Mon cadavre est doux comme un gant
   5. Violon
   6. Fleurs

1940

Banalités   (G. Apollinaire)   MAX ESCHIG
   1. Chanson d'Orkenise
   2. Hôtel
   3. Fagnes de Wallonie
   4. Voyage à Paris
   5. Sanglots

1942

Chansons villageoises   (Maurice Fombeure)
MAX ESCHIG
   1. Chanson du clair tamis

2. Les gars qui vont à la fête
3. C'est le joli printemps
4. Le mendiant
5. Chanson de la fille frivole
6. Le retour du sergent

1943

Métamorphoses　(Louise de Vilmorin)
SALABERT
1. Reine des mouettes
2. C'est ainsi que tu es
3. Paganini

Deux poèmes　(Louis Aragon)　SALABERT
1. C.
2. Fêtes galantes

1945

Montparnasse　(G. Apollinaire)　MAX ESCHIG

Hyde Park　(G. Apollinaire)　MAX ESCHIG

1946

Le pont　(G. Apollinaire)　MAX ESCHIG

Un poème　(G. Apollinaire)　MAX ESCHIG

Paul et Virginie　(Raymond Radiguet)　MAX ESCHIG

1947

Trois chansons de F. Garcia Lorca　HEUGEL
1. L'enfant muet
2. Adelina à la promenade
3. Chanson de l'oranger sec

. . . Mais mourir　(P. Éluard)　HEUGEL

Hymne　(Racine)　SALABERT

Le disparu　(Robert Desnos)　SALABERT

Main dominée par le cœur　(P. Éluard)　SALABERT

1948

Calligrammes (G. Apollinaire)   HEUGEL
  1. L'espionne
  2. Mutation
  3. Vers le Sud
  4. Il pleut
  5. La grâce exilée
  6. Aussi bien que les cigales
  7. Voyage

1949

Mazurka   (Louise de Vilmorin)   (dans:
  Mouvements de cœur)   HEUGEL

1950

La fraîcheur et le feu (P. Éluard)   MAX ESCHIG
  1. Rayon des yeux . . .
  2. Le matin les branches attisent . . .
  3. Tout disparut . . .
  4. Dans les ténèbres du jardin . . .
  5. Unis la fraîcheur et le feu . . .
  6. Homme au sourire tendre . . .
  7. La grande rivière qui va . . .

1954

Parisiana (Max Jacob)   SALABERT
  1. Jouer du bugle
  2. Vous n'écrivez plus?

Rosemonde   (G. Apollinaire)   MAX ESCHIG

1956

Le travail du peintre (P. Éluard)   MAX ESCHIG
  1. Pablo Picasso
  2. Marc Chagall
  3. Georges Braque

4. Juan Gris
5. Paul Klee
6. Joan Miró
7. Jacques Villon

Deux mélodies 1956   MAX ESCHIG
   1. La souris (G. Apollinaire)
   2. Nuage (Laurence de Beylié)

Dernier poème   (Robert Desnos)   MAX ESCHIG

1958

Une chanson de porcelaine   (P. Éluard)   MAX ESCHIG

1960

La courte paille   (Maurice Carême)   MAX ESCHIG
   1. Le sommeil
   2. Quelle aventure!
   3. La reine de cœur
   4. Ba, be, bi, bo, bu
   5. Les anges musiciens
   6. Le carafon
   7. Lune d'Avril

WORKS FOR VOICE AND INSTRUMENTS

1918–1919

Le Bestiaire or *Cortège d'Orphée*   (Guillaume
   Apollinaire)   with flute, clarinet, bassoon and
   string quartet   MAX ESCHIG

1932

Le Bal masqué   (Max Jacob)   Secular cantata,
   for baritone and chamber orchestra
   SALABERT

1942

Chansons villageoises   (Maurice Fombeure)
 with orchestral accompaniment
MAX ESCHIG

1961

La Dame de Monte-Carlo   (Jean Cocteau)
 Monologue for soprano and orchestra
RICORDI

CHANSONS

1918–1932

Toréador   (Jean Cocteau)   CHESTER

1934–1935

Quatre chansons pour enfants   (Jaboune)
ENOCH
  La tragique histoire du petit René
  Nous voulons une petite sœur
  Le petit garçon trop bien portant
  Monsieur Sans-Souci

1940

Les chemins de l'amour   (Jean Anouilh)
MAX ESCHIG

BIBLIOGRAPHY
compiled by Patrick Saul

ADÉMA, Marcel: *Apollinaire* (trans. Denise Folliot). 298 pp. London. Heinemann 1954.

BATHORI, Jane: *Les Musiciens que j'ai connus* (trans. Felix Aprahamian). In *Recorded Sound* 4, 6 and 15. 23 pp. London 1962 and 1964.

BLOCH, Francine: *Francis Poulenc — Phonographie*. Illus. 255 pp. Paris. Bibliothèque Nationale: Département de la Phonothèque Nationale et de l'Audiovisuel 1984.

BERNAC, Pierre: *Francis Poulenc, the man and his songs*. Illus. 233 pp. London. Gollancz 1977.
- *The Interpretation of French Song* (with translations of song texts by Winifred Radford). 338 pp. London. Cassell 1970. Gollancz 1976.
- *Poulenc's songs*. In *Recorded Sound* 18. 7 pp. London. April 1965.

COCTEAU, Jean: *Cock and Harlequin, notes concerning music* (translated by Rollo H. Myers) (with two monograms by Pablo Picasso). Illus. 57 pp. London. The Egoist Press 1921.

DANIEL, Keith W.: *Francis Poulenc, his artistic development and musical style*. 390 pp. Ann Arbor. UMI Research Press 1982.

GOLD, Arthur, and Robert Fizdale: *Misia, the life of Misia Sert*. Illus. 338 pp. New York. Knopf 1980; London. Macmillan 1982.

HELL, Henri: *Poulenc, musicien français*. Illus. 260 pp. Paris. Plon 1958.

JOURDAN-MORHANGE, Hélène: *Mes amis musiciens*. 232 pp. Paris. Les Editeurs Réunis 1955.

MILHAUD, Darius: *Notes sans musique*. Illus. 374 pp. Paris. René Julliard 1963. *Notes without Music* (trans. Donald Evans, ed. Rollo Myers). London. Calder & Boyars 1967.

Monnier, Adrienne: *The very rich hours of Adrienne Monnier, an intimate portrait of the literary and artistic life in Paris between the wars* (Trans. with introduction and commentary by Richard McDougall). 536 pp. London. Millington 1976.

Poulenc, Francis: *Correspondence 1915–63*. Illus. 276 pp. Paris. Éditions du Seuil 1967.
– *Entretiens avec Claude Rostand*. Illus. 225 pp. Paris. René Julliard 1954.
– *Emmanuel Chabrier*. Illus. 188 pp. Paris and Geneva. La Palatine 1961. (trans. Cynthia Jolly). Illus. 104 pp. London. Dennis Dobson 1982.
– *Moi et mes amis* (with Stéphane Audel). Illus. 200 pp. Paris and Geneva 1963. *My Friends and Myself* (trans. James Harding). Illus. 152 pp. London. Dennis Dobson 1978.

Roy, Jean: *Francis Poulenc: L'homme et son œuvre*. Illus. 190 pp. Paris. Seghers 1964.

PUBLISHER'S NOTE Since Patrick Saul compiled the above list in 1985 many new books on and by Poulenc have been published, adding considerably to the Poulenc bibliography.

Noizay from the air

Poulenc in his study at Noizay

Poulenc with his friend, the singer Suzanne Peignot

Poulenc with his friend, the singer Rose Dercourt-Plaut. He accompanied her frequently and his song *Nuage* is dedicated to her

Poulenc teaching
Mickey to cook

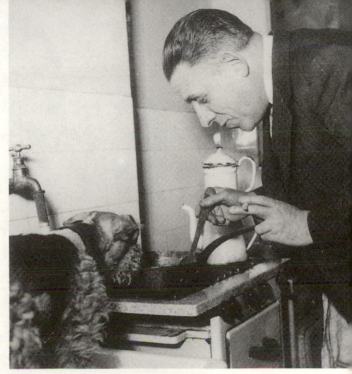

Poulenc
teaching Mickey
to play the piano
(These two
photographs
were taken by
Poulenc's young
nephew, Denis
Manceaux, who
died at an early
age)

Poulenc in uniform
at Cahors in 1940

Poulenc and Bernac
on board ship,
returning from a
tour in the U.S.A.

DISCOGRAPHICAL APPENDIX

by

PATRICK SAUL (1913-99) founder of the BIRS

THIS SELECTIVE DISCOGRAPHY, with notes on performers, is an attempt to document sound recordings which relate to people mentioned in Poulenc's *Journal* or which are of historical significance in relation to the performers of his vocal works.

Information about artists who have been associated with a composer is always of interest, and may be of value in helping to establish standards. For this reason — and to help readers to avoid a useless search — information is in some cases given about performers even if they are not known to have recorded works by Poulenc. For example, some of the singers whom he most admired unfortunately seem never to have recorded anything by him.

Alternative numbers for published records are not always given in full. For details of this kind and for information about Poulenc recordings in general readers should consult the *Phonographie de Francis Poulenc* listed in the bibliography above.

Abbreviations

BIRS   British Institute of Recorded Sound, now part of the British Library, and known as the British Library Sound Archive

HMV   His Master's Voice

INA   Phonothèque de l'Institut National de l'Audiovisuel, Paris

VSM   La Voix de son Maître

† signifies 78 rpm disc

★ signifies entry in *Discographical Appendix*

APOLLINAIRE, Guillaume (Wilhelm de Kostrowitzky) (1880–1918) French poet, of partly Polish extraction, natural son of Angelica Kostrowitzky; born in Rome but educated in France. Originally a Symbolist, but under the influence of Cubism and other modernist movements of the time he made experiments such as his *Calligrammes* (word-pictures), and became a leader of the avant-garde. His influence on poets of his own and later generations was immense.

Readers may judge for themselves whether they agree with Marie Laurencin's comment — mentioned by Poulenc in his *Journal* — on the affinity between Poulenc's songs and the sound of Apollinaire's voice by consulting the recordings made by the poet about 1911 for the Musée de la Parole of *Le Pont Mirabeau* and other poems. These are kept in the Phonothèque Nationale in Paris.

AURIC, Georges (1899–1983) French composer; member of "Les Six" (qv). A close friend of Poulenc, who dedicated to him *Cocardes*, 'Dans le jardin d'Anna', the Sinfonietta and the fifth *Improvisation pour piano*.

Auric was involved in many records including piano duets by Satie — *Parade* and two of the *Morceaux en forme de poire* — which he recorded with Poulenc about 1937 (Boîte à Musique 16/17†).

Auric's song 'Le Gloxinia' (text by René Chalupt) was recorded by Pierre Bernac accompanied by Poulenc (VSM DA 4893†; FALP 50036; C 061–12818; HMV COLH 151). See also under Pierre BERTIN, Louis DUREY, Darius MILHAUD and Yvonne PRINTEMPS.

BALGUERIE, Suzanne (1888–1973) French soprano; début at Opéra-Comique 1907 in Dukas's *Ariane et Barbe-bleue* (from which she recorded some arias (VSM W 577† and Columbia LFX 23†); at Paris Opéra until 1935; also had a distinguished career in the concert hall. Poulenc dedicated the 'Berceuse' from *Cinq Poèmes de Max Jacob* to her. She made no record of any work by him.

BATHORI, Jane (pseud. of Jeanne-Marie Berthier) (1877–1970) French singer and pianist; sang at the Scala, Milan under Toscanini in 1902; from about 1898 to 1939 gave performances of vocal works by most French composers of any importance, including first performances of songs by Debussy, Ravel, Poulenc ('Vocalise' in 1927 and *Airs chantés* in 1928) and many others. She directed the Théâtre du Vieux-Colombier while its founder Jacques Copeau was absent during the first world war; Poulenc dedicated the 'Air vif' from the *Airs chantés*, 'A son page' from *Poèmes de Ronsard* and 'Une Chanson de porcelaine' to her. This last song he wrote in homage to Mme Bathori on her 80th birthday.

She made no commercial records of works by Poulenc but to illustrate one of a series of talks which she gave for the British Institute of Recorded Sound in 1961, on Satie, "Les Six" and the "École d'Arcueil", she played the accompaniments for Louis-Jacques Rondeleux in 'Carte postale' (*Quatre Poèmes de Guillaume Apollinaire*), 'Voyage à Paris' (*Banalités*) and 'Rosemonde'. The talk and the illustrations are preserved in the Institute on tapes 371R and 374W/R.

See also under Francis POULENC for a talk which he recorded entitled *Hommage à Jane Bathori*; and under Les SIX.

BERNAC, Pierre (pseud. of Pierre Bertin: see note below) (1899–1979) French baritone and author. Pierre Bernac adopted this name because at the start of his career there was already a well-known actor-singer named Pierre Bertin (qv). Influenced as a young man by André Caplet (qv) and later by Yvonne Gouverné (qv) and (for Lieder interpretation) by Reinhold von Warlich; toured extensively as a concert singer; in 1926 was accompanied by Poulenc for the first time, in the première of the latter's *Chansons gaillardes*; in 1934 formed with Poulenc a duo for the performance of the songs of France and other countries which lasted until Bernac's retirement from the concert platform in 1960.

During the 25 years of the duo's existence Bernac was the first to sing a large proportion of Poulenc's new songs, many of which were dedicated to him.

From 1960 until his death Bernac taught song interpretation and lectured in France, Holland, Canada, the US and England, and he wrote books on *The Interpretation of French Song* and *Francis Poulenc, the man and his songs*.

In addition to the commercial records listed below, unpublished recordings which relate to Poulenc and which are known to exist include the following:

(a) in the INA: *Tel jour telle nuit* and *Chansons villageoises* (recorded 1952); *La Fraîcheur et le feu* (1953); *Tel jour telle nuit, Chansons villageoises, Quatre Poèmes de Guillaume Apollinaire*, 'C'est ainsi que tu es', 'Tu vois le feu du soir' and *Le Bestiaire* (1954); *Le Travail du peintre* (1959) all accompanied by Poulenc; ' . . . Mais mourir' (1953) with unnamed accompanist; *Chansons villageoises* (the composer's version with orchestral accompaniment) (1944) with orchestra conducted by Roger Désormière; *L'Histoire de Babar* (the version with orchestral accompaniment orchestrated by Jean Françaix) (1966) with orchestra conducted by Edgar Cosma.

(b) in the BIRS: *Le Travail du peintre, Tel jour telle nuit* and *La Fraîcheur et le feu* (all accompanied by Poulenc and taken from BBC broadcasts); lectures by Bernac (in English) on *The Interpretation of song* (1964; BIRS tapes 451/2), *Poulenc's songs* (1964; tapes 453/4) and *Poulenc* (1971; tape T.502W). Master classes conducted by Bernac (28 January to 3 February 1964) (tapes BIRS 699/711).

Commercial Records (all accompanied by the composer unless otherwise stated).

Ultraphone
BP 1531† recorded 1935 (reissue Rococo 5276). 'L'Anguille', 'Carte postale' and 'Avant le cinéma' from *Quatre Poèmes de Guillaume Apollinaire*.

VSM/HMV/Pathé–Marconi:

DA 4894† recorded 1936 (reissue Friends of Pierre Bernac PB3): 'Invocation aux parques' and 'La Belle jeunesse' from *Chansons gaillardes*

DB 6267† recorded 1945 (reissue Friends of Pierre Bernac PB3): *Métamorphoses* and *Deux Poèmes de Louis Aragon*

DB 6299† recorded 1945: *Le Bestiaire* (reissue Friends of Pierre Bernac PB3) 'Montparnasse' (reissues VSM FALP 50036; C 061–12818);

DB 6383/4† recorded 1946: *Tel jour telle nuit* (reissue Friends of Pierre Bernac PB3) 'Dans le jardin d'Anna' (reissue VSM FALP 50036; C 061–12818; HMV COLH 151)

Véga/Adès

Old couplings (C30A292/3 and C35A34/5) have been super-seded by Adès 7048/50 as listed below, the contents of the various sides being differently distributed. All the songs were recorded in 1958 or 1960.

7048 *Le Bestiaire*, 'Le Pont', 'Montparnasse', *Cinq Poèmes de Paul Éluard*, *La Fraîcheur et le feu*, 'Dans le jardin d'Anna' and 'Allons plus vite'

7049 'Épitaphe', *Chansons gaillardes*, 'Priez pour paix', 'Le Disparu', 'Tu vois le feu du soir', 'Paul et Virginie', 'La Grenouillère', *Parisiana*, 'C'est ainsi que tu es' and 'C'

7050 *Banalités*, *Tel jour telle nuit*, *Calligrammes* and *Le Travail du peintre*

14052 *Le Bal masqué* (with Francis Poulenc, piano, and instrumental ensemble conducted by Louis Frémaux) (re-corded under the artistic direction of the composer) (old numbers Véga C35A35; Westminster 18422; W 9618)

Columbia (US)

ML 4333 recorded 1951: *Banalités*, *Chansons villageoises* (also issued on CX 1119, FCX 141, Odyssey 32260009 and CBS 34031/2)

ML 4484 recorded 1952: *Quatre Poèmes d'Apollinaire*, 'Tu vois le feu du soir', 'Main dominée par le cœur' and *Calligrammes*

XLP 9280/1 recorded 1959 (unpublished tests): *Tel jour telle nuit*

Friends of Pierre Bernac.
PB1 recorded 27 November 1977 (BBC broadcast) (accompanied by Graham Johnson) *L'Histoire de Babar, le petit éléphant*
PB3 (reissue of VSM/HMV records listed above): *Le Bestiaire, Chansons gaillardes* 4 and 7, *Tel jour telle nuit, Deux Poèmes de Louis Aragon* and *Métamorphoses*

Pierre Bernac gave artistic guidance for the set of five VSM records containing all Poulenc's songs, accompanied by Dalton Baldwin and sung by Gérard Souzay (qv), Elly Ameling, Nicolai Gedda, William Parker and Michel Sénéchal (2C 165–16231/5)

See also under Georges AURIC, Charles GOUNOD and Darius MILHAUD.

BERTIN, Pierre (1895–1984) French actor, singer and playwright; at Théâtre de l'Odéon and Comédie Française 1923–45; also with Compagnie Jean-Louis Barrault; active in organizing concerts by "Les Nouveaux Jeunes" (the nucleus of "Les Six" (qv); with Jane Bathori (qv) he sponsored the concert on 11 December 1917 at the Vieux-Colombier at which the first public performance of a work by Poulenc — the *Rapsodie nègre* — took place. Poulenc dedicated 'Toréador' to Bertin.
Among Bertin's recordings are *Le Gendarme incompris* (Cocteau and Radiguet) with Jacques Hilling and Poulenc (piano) (unpublished recording of 1952 broadcast kept in the INA); and *Les Mariés de la Tour Eiffel*, a ballet with text by Cocteau and music by Auric, Honegger, Milhaud, Tailleferre and Poulenc, in a performance conducted by Darius Milhaud (Adès 15501; 14007). Bertin also made a record entitled *Monsieur Erik Satie* which contains an evocation of Satie and readings of extracts from Satie's writings including two letters to Valentine Hugo, *Étude su:*

les Embryons desséchés, *Mémoires d'un amnésique*, *Phrases*, *Conférence sur les animaux dans la musique* and *Marche du grand escalier* (Adès 4099).

See also under Louis DUREY.

BIZET, Georges (1838–75) French composer; his operas include *Les Pêcheurs de perles*, *La Jolie fille de Perth* and *Carmen*. Among his many other works he wrote about forty songs and duets. See under Reynaldo HAHN.

BOURDIN, Roger (1900–74) French baritone; career in opera (Paris Opéra from 1922) and in concert hall; gave first performance, in 1943, of *Chansons villageoises*. 'C'est le joli printemps' from this cycle was dedicated to him. He made no records of works by Poulenc.

BOURMAUCK, Ernest. French conductor. Poulenc dedicated 'Tristis est anima mea' from *Quatre Motets pour un temps de pénitence* to him. He conducted the Chanteurs de Lyon in the première of the Mass in G major in 1938, and they recorded the work (omitting the 'Qui tollis') in 1939 (Columbia RFX 61/2†).

CAPLET, André (1878–1925) French composer, conductor and pianist, who worked in close collaboration with Debussy. Pierre Bernac considered Caplet's *Forêt* to be one of the most beautiful of French songs. No records by Caplet himself have been traced.

See under Claire CROIZA.

CARTERI, Rosanna (*b.* 1930) French soprano. Mme Carteri made no published records of songs by Poulenc, but some recordings of broadcasts by her with Poulenc as accompanist are preserved in the INA: *Airs chantés*, the first performance of his *Gloria*, and an extract from *Dialogues des Carmélites*. She was the soloist in the published record of the *Gloria* conducted by Georges Prêtre with Yvonne Gouverné as chorus master (Columbia FCX 882; CX 1798; SAX 2445; HMV ASD 2835; 2C 069–12102).

CHABRIER, Emmanuel (1841–94) French composer. Poulenc's

devotion to Chabrier started when, as a boy, in the Paris showroom of the Pathé company, he heard the *Idylle* for piano, played on a record by Édouard Risler (Pathé 9533†) to whom Chabrier dedicated the *Bourrée fantasque*. Later Poulenc studied the piano with Ricardo Viñes, who had known Chabrier and often played his works. In 1961 Poulenc published *Emmanuel Chabrier*, a biographical and critical study. He recorded various works by Chabrier: the *Trois Valses romantiques*, with the pianist Marcelle Meyer (Discophiles Français 151/2; VSM C 151 73125/6) and some songs, accompanying Pierre Bernac: 'L'Île heureuse' and 'Ballade des gros dindons' (VSM DA 4892†; FALP 50036; COLH 151; C 061–12818); 'L'Île heureuse' and 'Villanelle des petits canards' (US Columbia ML 4484; Odyssey 32–26–0009; CBS 54031/2).

CHANTEURS DE LYON, Les. Commissioned *Sept Chansons*, and *Quatre Motets pour un temps de pénitence*, and gave the first performance of the former.
See also under Ernest BOURMAUCK.

CHEVALIER, Maurice (1888–1972) French singer, dancer, actor and author; début at twelve; partner of Mistinguett, Gaby Deslys and others; his international career lasted for more than 60 years; Poulenc often expressed his admiration for Chevalier, as did Bernac — for example in his master classes. Poulenc says in *Entretiens avec Claude Rostand* that his song 'Toréador' was strongly influenced by Chevalier's singing of the music hall song 'Si fatigué', of which Chevalier made a record in about December 1924 (Pathé 4181†; XR 181†; Salabert 175†).

COCTEAU, Jean (1889–1963) French poet, novelist, playwright, film director and artist. Propagandist for Picasso, "Les Six" (qv), Stravinsky and other causes. Among the many recordings in which he was involved is a discussion between him and Poulenc entitled *Du Groupe des Six au Bœuf sur le toit* broadcast in 1953 and kept in the INA.
See also under Marianne OSWALD and Edith PIAF.

CONRAD, Doda (pseud. of Doda Freund) (*b.* 1905) French bass of Polish extraction, son of Marya Freund (qv). At his request Poulenc wrote 'La Souris' for the birthday of Marya Freund. For him Poulenc also wrote 'Mazurka', a contribution to a set of six songs by various composers — the others being Auric, Milhaud, Sauguet, Françaix and Preger —commissioned by Conrad to celebrate the centenary of Chopin's death. Poulenc dedicated 'Hymne' to Conrad who, accompanied by David Garvey, gave the first performances of it and 'Mazurka' in New York in 1949. They recorded 'Mazurka' in 1950 on a commercial record (Robert E. Blake REB 2), and Conrad, with Jean Françaix as accompanist, recorded 'Hymne' for a French broadcast in 1965. This last recording is preserved in the INA, together with a performance of 'Livre' from *Sept Chansons*, in which Conrad is joined by Flore Wend, Violette Journeaux and Paul Derenne, dating from 1958.

Conrad is well known for the records by Nadia Boulanger's ensemble, of Monteverdi, Brahms and Rameau, in which he participated.

CROIZA, Claire (née Conelly) (1882–1946) French mezzo-soprano of Irish and Italian parentage; début 1905; at Théâtre de la Monnaie in Brussels from 1906; at Paris Opéra from 1908. Closely associated with many composers including Fauré (she sang the title role in his *Pénélope* at its first performance in Belgium), Saint-Saëns, d'Indy, Bréville, Duparc, Debussy, Roussel, Honegger and Caplet. Of Caplet she recorded 'Oraison dominicale' and 'Salutation angélique' from *Les Prières* (Lumen 32004†; 220015†).

Among Croiza's other records are songs by Bréville, Roussel and Honegger accompanied by the composers, and by Debussy, Duparc and Fauré accompanied by Poulenc. He also accompanied Croiza in *Le Bestiaire* on a record made in 1928 (Columbia D 15041†; COLC 317; Croiza Records CRO 1; HMV ALP 2115; VSM 2C 047–12538; C 051–14150).

Poulenc dedicated 'Je n'ai plus que les os' from *Poèmes de Ronsard* to Croiza. Of her Paul Valéry wrote "La voix la plus sensible de notre génération".

DERCOURT-PLAUT, Rose. (1890-1992) Polish-American soprano; pupil of Désiré Inghelbrecht; worked with Poulenc from 1949; he dedicated 'Nuage' to her. She recorded with Poulenc as accompanist (c.1956) 'Nuage'; *Cinq Poèmes de Paul Éluard; le Travail du peintre;* 'Air romantique' from *Airs chantés*; 'La Grenouillère'; *Huit Chansons polonaises* (in Polish); 'Avant le cinéma' from *Quatre Poèmes de Guillaume Apollinaire* (Turnabout (Vox) TV 4489)

DÉSORMIÈRE, Roger (1898–1963) French conductor and composer; member of the 'École d'Arcueil'; conducted premières of the 'Pastourelle' from *L'Éventail de Jeanne* (1927); *Les Animaux modèles* (1942); the Concerto for organ and orchestra (with Maurice Duruflé) (1939) and the Sinfonietta (1948).

He recorded for a broadcast with Pierre Bernac, in 1944, the version of *Chansons villageoises* with orchestral accompaniment, which is preserved in the INA, and also, about 1952, a commercial record of *Les Biches* suite (Decca LXT 2720; 592106; Ace of Clubs ACL 189; London LL 624).

DUBAS, Marie (1894–1972) French singer; début at 14; original career in operetta; at the Olympia music-hall in Paris in 1927 her singing of the song 'Pedro' (Rodor and Gey), described as a "fantaisie hispano-montmartroise", made her famous. Following the example of her idol, Yvette Guilbert, she included in her programmes folk songs, comic songs and songs of realism and tragedy. Of Marie Dubas Edith Piaf said "she was my model, the example that I wanted to follow". She made many records from 1924 onwards. A collection has been reissued which includes a 1927 recording of 'Pedro' and a tribute to her by Edith Piaf (Pathé – Marconi 2C 134–15406/7).

DUREY, Louis (1888–1979) French composer; a member of

"Les Six" (qv); became a communist. His Op. 17 consisted of settings of twenty-six poems from *Le Bestiaire* by Apollinaire, including all those set by Poulenc in his original 1919 publication and the 1956 publication of 'La Souris'.

A recording of a performance of Durey's *Le Bestiaire* by Lise Arséguet accompanied by Odette Pigault, made on 28 October 1965, is in the INA, which also possesses a recording of two of his settings — 'La Souris' and 'La Méduse' — made on 24 January 1969 by Pierre Bertin accompanied by Georges Auric.

DUVAL, Denise (*b.* 1923) French soprano; after singing at the Folies-Bergère music hall, Mme Duval went to the Opéra-Comique Petit Théâtre, where she was heard rehearsing *Tosca* by Max de Rieux. He spoke about her to Poulenc who invited her to sing the title role in *Les Mamelles de Tirésias*, the première of which took place in 1947. She recorded the work in 1953 (Columbia FCX 230; CX 1218; FCX 30351; Angel 35090; Seraphim 60029; VSM 2C 065–12510).

Poulenc dedicated *Dialogues des Carmélites* to her and she sang in the first performance of the original French version, in June 1957, under the direction of Pierre Dervaux; they recorded it later with all the other singers who had sung the principal roles at the first French performance — Denise Scharley, Régine Crespin, Rita Gorr and Liliane Berton (VSM FALP 523–5; 2C 153–12801/3; Angel 3585 C/L). (The world première, sung in Italian by Virginia Zeani and others, conducted by Nino Sanzogno, took place at the Scala, Milan on 26 January 1957, and a recording of that performance has been published (Legendary Recordings LR 144M). Mme Duval gave the first performance of *La Voix humaine* in 1959 and recorded it the same year, the conductor on both occasions being Georges Prêtre (Ricordi 30 CA 001; RCA LDS 2385; Vox OPL 160; VSM 2C–065–12052).

Poulenc's last song cycle, *La Courte paille*, was written for Mme Duval to sing to her young son, and was dedicated to

her and Richard Schilling. The first performance in public was given by Colette Herzog (qv), accompanied by Jacques Février.

The following broadcasts by Mme Duval with Poulenc at the piano are preserved in the INA: *Trois Poèmes de Louise de Vilmorin*; 'Main dominée par le cœur'; Air from the first tableau of *Dialogues des Carmélites*; First scene from *Les Mamelles de Tirésias*; 'Toréador' (all recorded in 1958). A recorded broadcast of *La Dame de Monte-Carlo*, sung by Mme Duval and conducted by Georges Prêtre, dating from 1961, is also in the possession of the INA.

FÉVRIER, Jacques (1900–79) French pianist; pupil of Édouard Risler and Marguerite Long; childhood friend of Poulenc. Février recorded a number of Poulenc's works for piano solo, and was artistic director of a set of the complete chamber works, in 13 of which he figured as the pianist (VSM 2C 165–12519/22).

He accompanied Gabriel Bacquier, Liliane Berton, Jean-Christophe Benoit and Michel Sénéchal in a record entitled *Poulenc et ses poètes*, dating from 1966 (Columbia CCA 1098).

See also under Colette HERZOG.

Poulenc wrote his Concerto in D minor for two pianos with Février's and his own styles of playing in mind and with a view to their playing it together. This they did at the première in Venice in 1932 and in two commercial records: the first of these was made in 1957 with Pierre Dervaux as conductor (Columbia FCX 677), and the second, made in 1962, with Georges Prêtre (VSM FALP 737; 2C 069–12100; HMV ALP 1967; ASD 517; Angel 35993).

FREUND, Marya (1876–1966) Polish singer resident in France; originally studied the violin with Sarasate; from the early years of the century she had a distinguished career as a singer of *Lieder* and of a wide variety of contemporary works, by Falla, Stravinsky, Schönberg, Ravel, Bloch, Prokofiev, Kodály, Poulenc and others. Poulenc dedicated 'La Souris',

'Le Tombeau' from the *Poèmes de Ronsard*, and 'Le Dernier mazour' from the *Chansons polonaises* to her. She recorded nothing by Poulenc, and none of her records has ever been published.
See under Doda CONRAD.

GIESEKING, Walter (1895–1956) German pianist, born in France of German parents. His repertoire embraced almost the entire piano literature, but he was revered especially for his interpretation of Debussy and Ravel. He was a master of pedal technique. Poulenc dedicated the *Humoresque* to him. He recorded nothing by Poulenc.

GOUNOD, Charles (1818–94) French composer. See under Reynaldo HAHN. Poulenc's own way of playing the accompaniments to Gounod's songs may be heard on records (Friends of Pierre Bernac PB 2 and PB 3 and VSM DA 4915; FALP 50036; C 061–12818; HMV COLH 151).

GOUVERNÉ, Yvonne (1890–1983) French chorus master and musicologist; pupil of Caplet, about whom she wrote a study under the pseudonym d'Yves-Marc. Conductor of the RTF (French Radio–Television) Choir from 1935. She was a close friend of Poulenc's and collaborated with him over a long period.
Recordings in the INA conducted by Mme Gouverné include: *Sept Chansons* (recorded 1959); *Figure humaine* (1959); *Litanies à la vierge noire* (1957); Mass in G major (1964); *Quatre Motets pour un temps de pénitence* (of which she was one of the dedicatees) (1966). The choir was also under her direction in recordings in the INA as follows: *Stabat Mater*, with Geneviève Moizan (qv), conducted by Manuel Rosenthal (1957); *Stabat Mater*, conducted by Georges Prêtre (1963); *Sept Répons des tenèbres*, conducted by Prêtre (1963). She was also chorus master in the commercial record of the *Gloria* conducted by Prêtre (Columbia FCX 882; CX 1798; SAX 2445; VSM 2C 069–12102; HMV ASD 2835).
She conducted the first performance of the *Quatre Petites*

prières de Saint François d'Assise but no recording of this work by her has come to light.

GREY, Madeleine (1897-1979) French soprano of Russian extraction; originally studied the piano, with Cortot; devoted herself to contemporary song; gave first performance of Ravel's *Chansons hébraïques* (which she recorded with the composer as accompanist) (Polydor 561075†; 62706†; Decca PO 5066†). She also recorded Ravel's *Chansons madécasses* with the instrumental accompaniment conducted by the composer (Polydor 561076/7†; Vox–Polydor 540008) and Canteloube's *Chants d'Auvergne*, which had been dedicated to her (Columbia LFX 27/9†; LCX 151/3†; ML4459; World Records SH 196). Two letters in Poulenc's correspondence (Dec 1937 and June 1938) indicate that she made a recording with Poulenc which, on the composer's advice, was not released.

HAHN, Reynaldo (1875–1947) French composer, singer, conductor and pianist of Venezuelan extraction; pupil of Massenet and Dubois; director of the Paris Opéra 1945; his songs, some of the best-known of which were written during his teens, and his operettas, especially *Ciboulette*, are the works on which his reputation rests.

The following records were made by Hahn of works by the composers whom Poulenc mentions in relation to him either as singer or accompanist or both: BIZET *Pêcheurs de perles*: 'De mon amie' (VSM 4–32078† recorded 1901–11); 'Chanson d'avril' and *Pêcheurs de perles*: 'Nadir doit expirer' (Columbia D 2021†; recorded 1927/8); GOUNOD 'Chanson de mai' (VSM 4–32073†; P 116† recorded 1901–11); 'Chanson de printemps' (VSM 4–32468†; P 405† recorded 1919); 'Biondina bella' (032397†; W 434† recorded 1919); 'Aimons-nous' (Columbia D 2020† recorded 1927–8); 'Maid of Athens' (Historic Masters HMB 14† recorded 1928). All these records are sung by Hahn; he accompanies

himself on Columbia D 2020/1 and probably does so on all the others.

HERZOG, Colette (1923–86) French singer. Gave the first performance of *La Courte paille* (which Poulenc wrote for Denise Duval (qv) to sing to her young son) at the Festival de Royaumont in 1960, accompanied by Jacques Février (qv). They recorded it and *Fiançailles pour rire* about 1963 (Deutsche Grammophon LPM 18882/SLPM 138882). With Anne-Marie de Lavilléon as accompanist Colette Herzog recorded 'Ce doux petit visage' in 1967 (Adès 13013).

HOROWITZ, Vladimir (1904–89) Russian pianist resident in the US. The early record which Poulenc mentions of Liszt's *Valse oubliée No. 1* was recorded in 1930 (HMV DA 1140†; Victor 1455†). In 1932 Horowitz recorded Poulenc's 'Pastourelle' from *L'Éventail de Jeanne* (in the composer's version for piano) and the 'Toccata' from *Trois Pièces pour piano* (HMV DB 2247†; COLH 300; VSM 2C 053–01902; 2C 061–01902). In 1951 he recorded the *Presto in B flat* (RCA 120428†; VSM DB 6971†; 491042 (45 rpm)) which was dedicated to him, as was the *Valse-Improvisation sur le nom de Bach*.

JOURDAIN-MORHANGE, Hélène (1892–1961) French violinist (pupil of Enesco and Capet) and critic. She was one of Ravel's closest friends and wrote a book entitled *Ravel et nous* about him; he dedicated his Violin Sonata to her.
As the leader of a string quartet she collaborated with Jane Bathori, Blaise Cendrars, Pierre Bertin and others in the concerts of "Les Nouveaux Jeunes", the nucleus out of which grew "Les Six" (qv). Poulenc dedicated 'Le Portrait' to her.

LANDOWSKA, Wanda (1879–1959) Polish harpsichordist, pianist and author. Poulenc dedicated to her 'La Vistule', from *Huit Chansons polonaises*, and the *Concert champêtre*. She gave the first performance of this last work in 1929 with the Orchestre Symphonique de Paris conducted by Pierre

Monteux. A recording of a performance of it which she gave in 1949 with the Philharmonic-Symphony Orchestra of New York under Leopold Stokowski has been published (International Piano Library IPL 106/7; Desmar IPA 106/7).

MILHAUD, Darius (1892–1974) French composer, pianist and conductor; member of "Les Six"; colleague and close friend of Poulenc. To celebrate Milhaud's return from America towards the end of the second world war Poulenc dedicated *Les Mamelles de Tirésias* to him. Among his best known works are *Le Bœuf sur le toit, La Création du Monde* and *Saudades do Brasil*. Milhaud made innumerable records of his own works; he also conducted a performance of *Les Mariés de la Tour Eiffel*, a ballet with text by Cocteau and music by Auric, Honegger, Poulenc and Milhaud himself. In this performance, recorded in 1966, Pierre Bertin and Jacques Duby are the two speakers (Adès 14007; 15501).
Pierre Bernac, accompanied by Poulenc, recorded Milhaud's *La Tourterelle* (text by Léo Latil) (VSM DA 4894†; FALP 50036; C 061–12818; HMV COLH 151).
See also under Francis POULENC for a recorded talk kept in the INA entitled *Hommage à Darius Milhaud*.

MODRAKOWSKA, Marya (1896–1965) Polish singer (pupil of Henry Melcer, H. Kedroff and Nadia Boulanger), critic and novelist; career in opera at Paris Opéra, Opéra-Comique (début as Mélisande 1932) and elsewhere, and in concert hall; taught at École Normale de Musique and, after 1938, in Cracow. On the occasion of a tour in North Africa in 1933, by Mme Modrakowska with Poulenc as accompanist, he harmonized for her the *Huit Chansons polonaises*; he dedicated number 8 ('Le Lac') to her. No records by Modrakowska have been traced.

MOIZAN, Geneviève. French soprano; sang in the première of the *Stabat Mater* at Strasbourg on 13 June 1951 under the direction of Fritz Münch; she sings in a recording of the same work with the RTF Choir (chorus master Yvonne

Gouverné) under Manuel Rosenthal, which is kept in the INA.

MORYN, Gilbert, baritone; gave the first performance of *Le Bal masqué* at Hyères, where the dedicatees, the Vicomte and Vicomtesse de Noailles, had a house, on 20 April 1932. No records by M. Moryn have been traced.

OSWALD, Marianne (pseud. of Marianne Colin) (1903–85) French singer; in cabaret in Berlin 1925; in Paris 1934. She specialized in songs of tragedy and revolt, with texts by Brecht, Prévert and others, including Cocteau, who wrote for her *La Dame de Monte-Carlo* — which Poulenc subsequently set to music for Denise Duval (qv) — and *Anna la Bonne* which she recorded with an announcement spoken by Cocteau himself (Columbia DF 1463†; Pathé 2 161–11311/2). Her style is also demonstrated by her record of Honegger's *Le Grand étang* (Columbia DF 1114†). She appears to have recorded nothing by Poulenc.

PEIGNOT, Suzanne (1895-1993) French soprano. Poulenc dedicated to her the 'Air champêtre' from *Airs chantés*; 'Attributs' from *Poèmes de Ronsard*; 'La Petite servante' from *Cinq Poèmes de Max Jacob*; and 'Il vole' from *Fiançailles pour rire*. Accompanied by Poulenc, she gave the first performances of *Le Bestiaire* in 1919; *Poèmes de Ronsard* in 1925; *Trois Poèmes de Louis Lalanne* in 1931; *Quatre Poèmes de Guillaume Apollinaire* in 1931; and 'Berceuse' and 'Souric et Mouric' from *Cinq Poèmes de Max Jacob* in 1932.
She recorded, with Poulenc at the piano, the *Airs chantés* in 1930 (Columbia LF5†; COLC 317; VSM 2C 047–12538). The following recordings of broadcasts by Mme Peignot, accompanied by Poulenc, are preserved in the INA: 'Je n'ai plus que les os' and 'Attributs' from *Poèmes de Ronsard*; *Cinq Poèmes de Max Jacob* (all recorded in 1945) and 'Paul et Virginie' (recorded in 1952).

PIAF, Edith (pseud. of Edith Giovanni Gasson) (1915–63) French singer, author and composer; as a child she sang in

the streets; there she was heard by Louis Leplée, the director of a night-club, where she made her real début; he named her "La Môme Piaf" (little sparrow). She was encouraged by Maurice Chevalier, and was influenced by various established singers, particularly Marie Dubas (qv) on whose style she modelled her own. Her strong personality, vibrant voice, her songs of fate and passion, also her own history, brought her enormous popularity. Cocteau wrote for her *Le Bel indifférent*, which she performed for the first time on 19 April 1940 at the Bouffes-Parisiens and later recorded (Pathé 2C 161–11311/12). She made many records, some of which have been brought together in collections (Polydor on Philips 6680258 and Columbia and Pathé on Pathé – Marconi 2C 150–72085/98). She recorded nothing by Poulenc. He dedicated his fifteenth *Improvisation pour piano, en ut mineur* to her in 1959.

POULENC, Francis (1899–1963) French composer, pianist and author. Poulenc made a large number of records of his works with piano — solos, concertos, instrumental combinations and of course accompaniments in vocal works. There are also a few recordings which do not fit into these categories. For example the records by Pierre Bernac (qv) of *Le Bal masqué* made "under the artistic direction of the composer". Some records also exist in which Poulenc speaks. These include *Ma musique est mon portrait* (recorded at his house at Noizay in 1962) (Disques Culturels Français 13) and the following recorded broadcasts in the INA: *Causerie sur Satie* (1949), *Souvenirs sur Raymond Radiguet* (1952), *Hommage à Jane Bathori* (1957), *Hommage à Darius Milhaud* (1960) and a conversation with Jean Cocteau entitled *Du groupe des Six au Bœuf sur le toit.* (1953).

An important recording in the INA is of a 1947 broadcast of *Rapsodie nègre*, the first of Poulenc's works to have been performed in public, in 1917. In the record the composer plays the piano, there is an unnamed vocalist (possibly Poulenc himself) and six other instrumentalists. For details

of an INA recording of *Le Gendarme incompris* in which Poulenc plays the piano see under Pierre BERTIN.

In the following recordings Poulenc plays the piano part: *L'Histoire de Babar, le petit éléphant*: with Pierre Fresnay (Discophiles Français DF 425105 recorded 1956), Cedric Belfrage (in English) (recording of BBC broadcast in the BIRS tape 697R) and Noel Coward (in English) (Aurore ABA 253 recorded about 1957 unpublished).

For records of his vocal works in which Poulenc is the pianist see under Pierre BERNAC, Rosanna CARTERI, Claire CROIZA, Rose DERCOURT-PLAUT, Denise DUVAL, Suzanne PEIGNOT and Geneviève TOURAINE. For records on which Poulenc accompanies songs by other composers see under AURIC, CHABRIER, GOUNOD, MILHAUD, ROUSSEL and SATIE. With regard to Poulenc's comments in the *Journal* on neglect of the original version, for voice and orchestra, of *Le Bestiaire*, various records have been made, including the following: Irène Joachim (soprano) with orchestra conducted by Maurice Franck (Chant du Monde LDA; LDX 78410) and by Jean-Jacques Benoit (baritone) conducted by Georges Prêtre (VSM FALP 869; HMV ALP/ASD 2296).

PRÊTRE, Georges (*b.* 1924) French conductor. Has given many performances and made many records of works by Poulenc including the première of *La Voix humaine*. Among his records the following are of vocal works: *La Voix humaine* and *La Dame de Monte-Carlo* (both with Denise Duval (qv)); the *Gloria* (with Rosanna Carteri (qv)); *Le Bal masqué*, *Le Bestiaire*, *Chansons villageoises* and *Rapsodie nègre* (all with Jean-Jacques Benoit (baritone) (VSM FALP 869; HMV ALP/ASD 2296); the *Stabat Mater* (see under Yvonne Gouverné); *Quatre Motets pour un temps de pénitence* (VSM PALP 789; 2C 069–12016; HMV ASD 583).

PRINTEMPS, Yvonne (1894–1977) French singer and actress; married to Sacha Guitry from 1919–32; later to Pierre Fresnay. She made two records of songs by Poulenc: 'Les Chemins de l'amour' from *Léocadia* (a comedy by Jean

Anouilh) (VSM DA 4927†; FDLP 1088; FKLP 7004; 2C 064–10811; recorded 1940) and 'A son guitare' from *Margot* (a comedy by Édouard Bourdet, the poem of 'A son guitare' being by Ronsard); it is coupled on the original 78 rpm record with Auric's *Printemps*, also from *Margot* (VSM DA 4879†; FALP 50040; recorded 1935); all these songs are accompanied by the Orchestre Marcel Cariven. Poulenc dedicated both his songs to Yvonne Printemps.

RADIGUET, Raymond (1903–23) French poet and novelist who lived with and was a protégé of Cocteau. See under Pierre BERTIN and for recorded talk about him under POULENC.

RONSARD, Pierre de (1524–85) French poet of courtly love. See under Yvonne PRINTEMPS.

ROUSSEL, Albert (1869–1937) French composer; originally a naval officer; studied with Gigout and Vincent d'Indy; among his pupils were Satie and Varèse. He wrote four symphonies, the opera *Padmâvati, Évocations* for orchestra with chorus, about 35 songs, various piano and chamber works and, his best known composition, the ballet *Le Festin de l'araignée.*

In spite of the criticisms which Poulenc directs at some of Roussel's songs, he recorded (with Geneviève Touraine) 'Ode à un jeune gentilhomme', 'Amoureux séparés' and 'Cœur en péril' (Boîte à Musique LD 012) and (with Pierre Bernac) 'Cœur en péril' and 'Le Jardin mouillé' (VSM DA 4918†; FALP 50036; C 061–12818; COLH 151).

SATIE, Erik Alfred Leslie (1866–1925) French composer whose mother was Scottish; an eccentric; friendly with Debussy; a group of young composers ("Les Six" (qv)) formed round him; Cocteau, who collaborated with him in a ballet for Diaghilev called *Parade*, waged a propaganda campaign on his behalf; later a second group of young composers, known as the "École d'Arcueil" after the district where Satie lived, allied themselves to him — Henri Sauguet (qv),

Roger Désormière (qv), Henri Cliquet-Pleyel and Maxime Jacob.

Poulenc was fascinated by Satie from an early age, at first by the fantastic titles which he gave to his compositions — for example, *Morceaux en forme de poire*, *Prélude flasque pour un chien* and *Avant-dernières pensées* — and later when he met him at Ricardo Viñes' house. Poulenc recorded various piano solos by Satie (Columbia ML 4399; Odyssey Y 33792; CBS 61838; also Boîte à Musique LD 023; LD 5744; LD 5866) and duets played with Jacques Février (Club Français du Disque 272/3; Musidisc RC 16018) and also with Georges Auric (qv). Poulenc also recorded some of his songs with Pierre Bernac: 'La Statue de bronze' and 'Le Chapelier' from *Trois Mélodies* (VSM DA 4893†; Friends of Pierre Bernac PB 2) and the complete set — 'La Statue de bronze', 'Le Chapelier' and 'Daphénéo (Columbia ML 4484; Odyssey 32–26–009; CBS 54031/2).

SAUGET, Henri (1901-89) French composer; member of the "École d'Arcueil" and hence loyal to the ideals of Satie (qv). He was a pupil of Canteloube and a protégé of Milhaud's; has written music in all forms, including many songs; his best known works are *La Chatte*, a ballet written for Diaghilev; *Les Forains*, a ballet, a suite from which Sauguet himself conducted on record (Polydor 566254/6†; Philips S 05800; Chant du Monde LDXS 8300); *La Voyante*, a cantata (Germaine Cernay, soprano, and orchestra conducted by Roger Désormière) (Oiseau–Lyre OL 137/8†); *Visions infernales* (text by Max Jacob) (Louis-Jacques Rondeleux, baritone, accompanied by the composer) (Boîte à Musique LD 042); incidental music to *Ondine*, a play by Giraudoux; and an opera *La Chartreuse de Parme*. Poulenc dedicated 'Le Disparu' to him. Henri Sauguet played the piano accompaniments in a recording by Paul Derenne (tenor) of Poulenc's ' . . . Mais mourir', 'Voyage à Paris' from *Banalités*, 'Tu vois le feu du soir' from *Miroirs brûlants*, 'C' from *Deux Poèmes de Louis Aragon*, and 'Toréador'; this

recording dates from 1959 and is kept in the INA.
Henri Sauguet is President of the "Association des Amis de Francis Poulenc".

SIX, Les. During the first world war the composers Auric (qv), Durey (qv) and Honegger were associated with Cendrars, Cocteau, Apollinaire and others in evenings devoted to music and poetry readings. The group, inspired by Satie (qv), was known as "Les Nouveaux Jeunes", and for some years it organized concerts with such artists as Jane Bathori (qv), Suzanne Peignot (qv), Ricardo Viñes, Pierre Bertin (qv) and his wife Marcelle Meyer, and the Hélène Jourdan-Morhange String Quartet (qv). The original three composers were joined by Germaine Tailleferre (qv), Darius Milhaud (qv) and Poulenc and, in 1920, were called "Les Six" by the critic Henri Collet; this was a reference to "The Five" — the group of Russian composers who rejuvenated the music of their country. Cocteau acted as propagandist for the group.

SOUZAY, Gérard (pseud. of Gérard Michel Tisserand) (1918-2004) French baritone; studied with Pierre Bernac, Claire Croiza and others; distinguished career in opera and concert hall. Poulenc dedicated 'Chanson de l'oranger' from *Trois Chansons de F. Garcia Lorca* to Souzay. Souzay has made many records of works by Poulenc during his career, the earliest being a 1949 record accompanied by Jacqueline Bonneau of *Le Bestiaire* and 'Reine des mouettes' from *Métamorphoses* (Boîte à Musique BAM 63†). There are no recordings in which Poulenc himself accompanies Souzay.
In his *Journal* Poulenc praises Souzay's interpretation of two of his songs in particular; both of these he recorded with accompaniments played by Dalton Baldwin: in 1969 they recorded 'Priez pour paix' (Philips 02324; 835201; SAL 3480; PHM 511132) and in 1968 'Le Portrait' (RCA LM/ LCS 3018; 644515; SB 6782).
Souzay and Baldwin included new recordings of these two

songs in a set of five records containing all Poulenc's songs, sung by various singers, recorded under the guidance of Pierre Bernac (qv) (VSM 2C 165–16231/5). The songs in this set recorded by Souzay and Dalton are as follows: 'Priez pour paix'; 'Le Portrait'; *Le Bestiaire*, *Chansons gaillardes*; 'Épitaphe'; *Quatre Poèmes de Guillaume Apollinaire*; *Cinq Poèmes de Paul Éluard*; 'La Grenouillère'; *Chansons villageoises*; *Métamorphoses*; 'Hymne'; *Trois Chansons de Garcia Lorca*; 'Le Disparu'; 'Main dominée par le cœur'; 'Mazurka'; 'Parisiana'; *Le Travail du peintre*; 'La Souris'; 'Nuage'; 'Dernier poème'; 'Colloque' (duet with Elly Ameling). These recordings were made between 1974 and 1977.

STRAVINSKY, Igor (1882–1971) Russian composer, resident for many years in Paris and later in the US. There is a 1945 record in the INA of *Les Noces*, conducted by Manuel Rosenthal, in which Poulenc is one of the four pianists.

TAILLEFERRE, Germaine (1892–1983) French composer and pianist; member of "Les Six" (qv); studied at the Paris Conservatoire; her Sonata for violin and piano was played by Thibaud and Cortot and her Piano Concerto by Cortot. A set of *Six Chansons françaises* was recorded by Jane Bathori (soprano) accompanied by the composer (Columbia LF 53†). Poulenc's *Valse in C major* for piano was recorded by Mme Tailleferre in 1954 and she accompanied Bernard Lefort (baritone) in Poulenc's *Banalités*, *Le Bestiaire*, *Chansons villageoises* and 'Montparnasse' in a broadcast dating from 1953. These recordings are kept in the INA.

TOURAINE, Geneviève. French soprano; sister of Gérard Souzay. Poulenc dedicated 'L'Enfant muet' from *Trois Chansons de Garcia Lorca* to her. He accompanied her in *Fiançailles pour rire* and *Trois Chansons de Garcia Lorca* (together with songs by Roussel (qv) and Debussy) in a record made in 1954 (Boîte à Musique LD 012; LD 5744; LD 5866). She also recorded Poulenc's 'C', from *Deux Poèmes de Louis Aragon* and 'Reine des mouettes' and 'C'est ainsi que

tu es' from *Métamorphoses*, accompanied by Jacqueline Bonneau (Lumen LD 3402; recorded in 1955).

VALLIN, Ninon (pseud. of Eugénie Vallin-Pardo) (1886–1961) French soprano; great international career in opera and the concert hall; closely associated with Debussy (who often accompanied her at recitals), Reynaldo Hahn and Joaquin Nin (both of whom accompanied her on records of their songs). She made many records but none of songs by Bizet or of any work by Poulenc. Poulenc dedicated 'Mon cadavre est doux comme un gant', from *Fiançailles pour rire*, to her.

VILMORIN, Louise de (1902–72) French poet and novelist; her poems were — in the words of Pierre Bernac — "charming and elegant". She came of a family of horticulturalists, celebrated for the flowers and seeds that were grown on their estate at Verrières-le-Buisson. She recorded her poem 'Aux officiers de la garde blanche' (Decca 133614), which is the text of one of Poulenc's *Trois Poèmes de Louise de Vilmorin*.

WOODGATE, Leslie (1902–61) British conductor. A recording was made by the BBC of the first performance of the *Figure humaine* which took place (in an English translation by Rollo Myers) in January 1945 by the BBC Choir conducted by Leslie Woodgate.

★

ACKNOWLEDGMENTS

Details of first performances of some of Poulenc's works have been reprinted by courtesy of UMI Research Press from *Francis Poulenc: his artistic development and musical style* © 1982, 1980.

The information about unpublished Poulenc recordings preserved by the Phonothèque de l'Institut National de l'Audiovisuel, Paris (INA) is reprinted from the *Poulenc phonographie* by Francine Bloch by kind permission of the Bibliothèque Nationale (Département de la Phonothèque Nationale et de l'Audiovisuel) © 1984.

Particulars of these two books are given in the Bibliography on page 135.